LOSING A CHILD

LINDA HURCOMBE taught English Literature for 27 years at both university and secondary levels. She is co-author, with Susan Dowell, of *Dispossessed Daughters of* *...* (published by SPCK) and author/editor of *Sex and God* (Routledge). In recent years she has combined writing with editing and was co-ordinating editor of *The New Dictionary of Pastoral Studies* (SPCK, 2002), and editor of *Compassion*, the quarterly journal of The Compassionate Friends UK, from 2001 to 2004. She is the mother of two children – Caitlin, and a surviving older brother, Sean – and lives in Shropshire.

ALIS

2665156

Losing a Child

Explorations in Grief

Linda Hurcombe

sheldon **PRESS**

First published in Great Britain in 2004 by
Sheldon Press
1 Marylebone Road
London NW1 4DU

© Linda Hurcombe 2004

All rights reserved. No part of this book may be reproduced
or transmitted in any form or by any means, electronic or
mechanical, including photocopying, recording, or by any
information storage and retrieval system, without permission
in writing from the publisher.

British Library Cataloguing-in-Publication Data

A catalogue record for this book is available from the British Library

ISBN 0–85969–886–6

1 3 5 7 9 10 8 6 4 2

Typeset by Deltatype Limited, Birkenhead, Merseyside
Printed in Great Britain by Biddles Ltd
www.biddles.co.uk

ABERDEENSHIRE LIBRARY AND
Hurcombe, Linda
INFORMATION SERVICES

Losing a child
: explorations
in grief /

155.
937

2665156

Contents

In memory of Caitlin Elizabeth Rosalie Hurcombe,
11 June 1978–6 April 1998,
whose life made this book possible
and whose death made it mandatory.

And to The Compassionate Friends all around the world.

From the Safe Harbor Group:

> May I become at all times, both now and forever,
> a protector for those without protection
> a guide for those who have lost their way
> a ship for those with oceans to cross
> a bridge for those with rivers to cross
> a sanctuary for those in danger
> a lamp for those who need light
> a place of refuge for those needing shelter
> and a servant to all those in need.
>
> (The Dalai Lama)

Acknowledgements

Here are just some of the peerless companion explorers who have made this book possible: Trish Johnson, soul mate, Dr David Healy, soul friend, who believed me and then provided a compass for the expedition, Maria Hayes, whose bolthole in Ireland enabled the book's completion, my son Sean Hurcombe, Pat Neil (TCF), Jean Taylor – CRUSE, Dwayne Steffes – CRUSE, Dr Jill Gray, Judy Harper, Catharine Pointer (TCF Librarian), Michael Pointer, Linda Haines, Richard Tunnicliffe, Lisa Beznosiuk and Luba Mai Tunnicliffe, who bring friendship to life and music to the soul, Ron, Lynn and Amy Hester, Michael Wherly, Hillary Ratna, Lawrence Ratna, Val Bond and Betty Saunders, Pete Postlethwaite OBE and Jacqui Moorish, Ian Millward (Caitlin's teacher and co-founder of Caitlin's Kickstart Award), Kay Kershaw, Mike and Linda McKeen, Ann Marie McKeen and Venice, Jenny Morgan, Nikki Stockley, Vicky Marriott, Olga Edridge, Ramo Kabbani, Dr Una Kroll, Graham and Sue Dowell, Clare, Dominic, Barnaby and Benjamin Dowell, Professor Malcolm Brown and Heather Ferguson-Brown, Dr Gordon Riches, Dawn Rider, Gina Ross Vickery, Andy Vickery, Kathryn Wolfendale, Linda Crosby, Yolande Clarke, my agent Pat White. Finally, Joanna Moriarty, my brilliant editor, who cajoled and encouraged all the way.

'Precious Child' was written and sung by Karen Taylor-Good. Visit www.karentaylorgood.com for more information about Karen and her music. Special thanks to Roger McGough for permission to publish 'Sad Music', which first appeared in *Everyday Eclipses*, Viking, London, 2002. And to John Marsden, for *A Message for the 21st Century*, Ticktock Publishing, The Offices in the Square, Hadlow, Tonbridge TN11 0DD, 1998 (originally published in Australia by Thomas C. Lothian).

'The Mother', by Gwendolyn Brooks, first appeared in *A Street in Bronzeville*, published by Harper & Brothers in 1945. Used by permission.

Thanks to Lin Baldwin for permission to publish 'Grief'. This poem is part of a collection, *Calling Owls*, copies of which are available from Angel House, Milo, Llandybie, Ammanford, Carmarthenshire SA18 3NJ.

And thanks to Linda Baxter for permission to print 'For Our Spiritual Warrior' from her forthcoming book *Losing Timo*, to be published in 2005 by Hanno Welsh Women's Press.

Foreword

How do parents survive the death of a child?

Some don't. Heartbreak can be enough to take away the will to live. Guilt can bring the message that the bereaved person has no right to exist. Fortunately, most parents go on living.

Some parents go on living because, despite the pain, their bodies go on working, because they have other children to care for, because while they live their lost child is remembered. Some parents go on living because the nature of their child's death gives them a task which they feel the necessity to perform with all their might.

With the death of her daughter Caitlin, Linda Hurcombe found herself with two tasks to carry out. The first was to question the safety and effectiveness of the antidepressant Caitlin was taking before she died. The second task was to tell the truth about what follows for parents when their child dies.

In the attempt to make our difficult lives more bearable, we protect ourselves from reality. Another person's grief distresses us, and so we encourage that person to bear their grief 'well' – which actually means not displaying their grief in any way. Widows are often complimented with the statement, 'She's taking it well,' and some women do bear the death of their husband with enormous equanimity. To offer the same compliment to a bereaved parent, however, can give only pain and insult.

We might be able to accept the sight of a parent's grief, but protect ourselves from too much discomfort by taking the long view – that grief is a learning process from which the bereaved can graduate with 'closure'. We may hold firmly to the most comforting concept of all, that we live in a 'just world' where, if we suffer, we will eventually, and inevitably, receive recompense and reward.

None of these beliefs is true. When we grieve for someone we love we are broken into pieces, and some of those pieces go missing, never to be replaced. We want to scream our pain and confusion to the heavens. To be forced to be well behaved is torture. Over time our grief may become more muted, but it never goes away. We never become whole. That terrible absence is with us until we die, and for this terrible absence there is no recompense, no reward.

If we do not acknowledge these truths we cannot help others bear their grief, nor can we bear our own grief. Instead we feel guilty because we have apparently failed to deal with our grief in the way that we should. We have not found 'closure', nor have we been recompensed and rewarded.

Linda Hurcombe has confronted these truths through her own grief, and is able to write about them very directly and clearly. Moreover, she discovered that the death of your child does not protect you from the practical issues of living. Indeed, the grieving parent may be quite unprepared for the practical issues that do arise, and Linda includes in her compassionate account of parental grief much practical information and advice.

This is a book of great humanity and warmth. Reading it you will discover another great truth – that, while grief can isolate us, sorrow can bring us closer together than happiness ever can.

Dorothy Rowe

Introduction: Footprints in Snow

We fall to the earth like leaves
Lives as brief as footprints in snow
No words express the grief we feel
I feel I cannot let her go.

For she is everywhere.
Walking on the windswept beach
Talking in the sunlit square.
Next to me in the car
I see her sitting there.

At night she dreams me
and in the morning the sun does not rise.
My life is as thin as the wind
And I am done with counting stars.

She is gone, she is gone.
I am her sad music, and I play on, and on, and on.

(Roger McGough)

I began this book in the days preceding and immediately following the catastrophe of 11 September 2001, or '9/11' as it came to be known, when terrorist attacks on the twin towers of the World Trade Center in New York City and the Pentagon in Washington DC altered all our futures. Seasoned observers say we will always remember with precision what we were doing on this day, the way an earlier generation recalls the assassination of President John F. Kennedy in November 1963, the way my students and friends spoke of Princess Diana's fatal car crash in August 1997. This forms the 'big picture' and, as it happens, an appropriate context in which to write a book for people suffering huge loss, our intimate 9/11s.

I didn't want to write my personal story in this book. I wanted to write your stories. There is, however, a personal picture focusing on family tragedy and on my daughter Caitlin, and I cannot imagine that this is the book I'd be writing if she had not died. It is, I realize, entirely appropriate that Caitlin's story has become a leitmotif throughout.

Like many little girls in the 1980s, Caitlin grew up with daily images of the Princess of Wales, and adored her. Prompted by a kindergarten teacher, five-year-old Caitlin wrote a letter to the princess, accompanied by a drawing of Charles and Diana; it was later published in a book of children's letters. 'Dear Princess Diana, What do you like best about Buckingham Palace? Love, Caitlin Hurcombe aged five years.' Over the years, Caitlin continued to enjoy collecting occasional 'Diana mementos', adoring this royal icon with countless millions of others.

When Diana died so suddenly in August 1997, Caitlin shared the national sense of numbness and loss: 'How sad, Mum, without Diana in this world.' But, of course, life went on without Diana; college and boyfriends and simple ordinary affairs gradually fell into place.

There is no causal connection between the public tragedy of Diana's death and Caitlin's death eight months later. Caitlin died by suicide on the Monday of Holy Week, 6 April 1998, changing the lives for ever of those who loved her. She was 19 years old, two months away from her twentieth birthday. Were she alive today, I would – when required – be supply teaching at her sixth-form college, making the occasional broadcast, editing theological works and writing novels, and of course fretting and rejoicing over the ensuing stages of her growth to adult years – boyfriends, adventures, career – all the usual experiences that became excruciating 'what-ifferies' after her death.

Caitlin's story

Caitlin and her elder brother Sean were much loved and loving, and Caitlin grew into a normal self-conscious complicated teenager. Her clergyman father and I separated when she was nine years old, and it was necessary to move away to our rural home in Shropshire where, in spite of the considerable pain involved in the break-up of our previous family unit, Caitlin settled in well. For a time she had a pony called Julie, until 'Julie interest' was supplanted by 'boy interest'. Her priorities were friends, regular contact with her father and big brother in London, drama and singing, physical appearance, clothes, and 'sorting Mum out', by which I mean engaging in huge debates over virtually everything, conducted most often in the kitchen. Caitlin frequently won these verbal sparring matches with Mum. She would have made a superb lawyer. Friends, though, never seemed to see this pugilistic Caitlin, and would comment on how endlessly biddable and easy-going she was with them.

Her sixth-form years were safe and loving, if turbulent. 'You're always there for me, Mum,' she'd tell me in regular generous moments. I need to remember these moments, not least as reassurance that I did indeed let her know how much she meant to me. She was also the kind of girl who told me every single day that she loved me, sometimes even in the midst of an argument: 'Mum, you are such a moody Trudy! Get a grip! Love you!' she'd say, with the 'Love you' shouted over her shoulder as off she'd swoop to make a phone call or wash her hair.

During the unspeakable days following her death I clearly remember thinking, 'How will all the people I cherish be able to deal with the person I have become, will become?' There was life with Caitlin, and now life without her. All the many roads that led to Caitlin became cul-de-sacs. I harboured a terror that her older brother would follow her inexplicable exit from life. I felt a profound kinship with all lost needlessly dead children, and their surviving loved ones. Above all, there was a diminishment to such a degree that life appeared to lose all meaning. Writing – my 'almost way of making a living' – was out of the question. What was the point of words when there was no Caitlin in the world? I was dragged into a vortex of despair, where all I had worked for came to nothing. This sense of loss remains a personal struggle in spite of an abiding faith in God (not your fault, God!), a miraculous loving companion, the reward of work itself, and a grand extended family of true friends – you know who you are.

The following sequence of events is factual and chronologically accurate, although I have changed some names.

Caitlin wanted to take the antidepressant drug Prozac (the oldest and best known version of a group of medications known as selective serotonin reuptake inhibitors or SSRIs) because she felt 'down' after a difficult Christmas, and she wanted to lose weight. Friends told her that the drug was good on both counts. She informed the doctor she saw (not her own GP) that she was depressed and was prescribed the medication. In her diary Caitlin numbered her first and all subsequent days as 'PZ days'. At the end of the first day on the drug she skipped into the house from college saying she felt 'mega-great', which was a surprise because both the doctor and the 'Patient's Notes' emphasized that the medication might take at least a fortnight, and possibly more, to 'kick in'. I gave one of my mini-lectures about the placebo effect, and insisted on reading the Patient's Notes aloud to Caitlin. A separate set of instructions, logoed with a Crystal Mark of clarity from the Plain English Campaign, and titled 'Day by Day: A guide to your first three weeks of treatment', urged the patient to carry on with the drug no matter how bad they might feel.

Caitlin's 'day one' euphoria was short-lived, and by the first weekend on her medication she began complaining of a stiff jaw and of feeling 'edgy'. She began chewing her cheeks in her sleep, and while awake she couldn't settle.

That weekend, she went out with friends to a local pub. Later that night and at home, Caitlin was agitated and upset. She told me that she didn't know what had got into her, but she'd 'lost the plot', got into the flat of a local man called Psycho, and removed his stereo.

'Beg pardon?' I was dumbfounded. Psycho's nickname is not a term of endearment; his day job is at an abattoir cleaving beef carcasses. He also goes berserk at the drop of a hat or too many drops of alcohol.

'Where's the stereo, Cakes?' I asked.

'In my bedroom.'

'Your BEDROOM?'

'Listen. He's been slagging me off, Mum, so I thought I'd teach him a lesson – it's better than punching his lights out, which is what I wanted to do.'

The image of my gorgeous girl attempting to 'punch Psycho's lights out' was more scary than amusing. 'Get that stereo back into his house. I don't care how you do it.'

And she did. By the time the police arrived at Psycho's flat the next day to investigate the reported theft, Psycho's stereo was back *in situ*, cosily plugged in and ready to play, as if it had never been moved.

During college half-term Caitlin visited her father and brother Sean in London. Sean noticed she was very 'manic', and urged her to 'chill'. He instinctively cautioned her not to mix alcohol with her medication. This caveat later provoked a huge argument with me on her return home: I suggested that she moderate her intake and stop trying to 'keep up' with her mates. Caitlin retorted, 'If you aren't supposed to drink alcohol while on the drug, the Patient's Notes would say so, and there IS no warning. You read the instructions out loud to me, Mum, remember? Boring!! They would tell you like they do on antibiotic prescriptions. Right?' Caitlin ten, Mum nil. Otherwise she seemed happy, happy, happy. Through the vantage point of the 'retrospectoscope', much too happy.

Shortly after this period of 'euphoria' Caitlin woke me at three in the morning, crying in anguished sobs from her bedroom. I ran to her room.

'Mum, I dreamed you were dead!' I cuddled her and tried to talk her down from the nightmare.

'But Mum, I killed you with a machete.'

I managed a feeble joke. 'Well, most kids feel like killing their parents some of the time, honey.'

A couple of nights later she woke me again, having a nightmare in which she killed herself. Such was the violence of the dream that Caitlin was unable to go back to sleep that night. I stayed with her. Sleep disturbances continued.

A few days later Caitlin said, 'Mum, one thing I notice about being on Prozac is that like, I can't cry even when I want to. I either feel like, calm and floaty like, or I feel like, massively angry, but, like, in a calm sort of way.'

Instead of responding to what should have been a warning about the effect of the medication, my reaction to Caitlin's observation was to ignore her concerns, and ask her not to use 'like' so much. I did re-read the Patient's Notes, though, and was somewhat reassured that they said not to worry if the depressed person was still feeling bad, as they remained on the road to recovery as long as they carried on with the medication.

Although she was a distinction student, Caitlin became convinced that college teachers were marking her down. She charged into their empty office one day and commandeered the class register. At home she raged furiously, convinced that her tutors planned to fail her. I went with her into college to visit her head of department and sort things out. Her tutor seemed bemused, defensive and incredulous, quite naturally objecting to Caitlin's unprecedented behaviour. He produced the register and pointed out that she had looked at the wrong row of marks, that she was maintaining her distinction standard, but that he was concerned with her recent out-of-character and erratic behaviour. Caitlin, who normally would have apologized unreservedly to her teachers, seemed both unrepentant and unfeeling. It was like seeing another person acting inside her skin; the biblical term 'possessed' springs to mind. This change is made clear in a ferociously rude and vitriolic poem Caitlin wrote and circulated, extracted here (I have changed the names):

Ballad

There once were two teachers
Called Larry and Whim,
One was a wanker, the other, just dim.
They'd failed in their lives as actor and dancer,
Rude comments to students cut like a lancer ...

Remember those trousers?
Remember that belt?
Remember how much her egg sandwiches smelt?
Remember the good times?
No we do not.
Do it again? We'd rather chew snot.

This language, from a girl whose watchword was kindness, who was surrounded by friends and gifted teachers of whom she was extremely fond.

As suggested by the doctor she saw when Prozac was prescribed, Caitlin talked a counsellor who concluded that she was coping exceptionally well. Over tea that evening, Caitlin was elated.

'Mum, the counsellor says I'm psychologically intact!'

'Of course you are, darling.' Huge hugs.

And indeed there were productive days. During this time Caitlin co-wrote and produced a play based on a lighthearted look at the Seven Deadly Sins, called *Hell's Belles*. Even if I hadn't been a doting parent, I would have called it topnotch. On Mother's Day she presented me with an elaborately festooned box filled with brightly coloured primroses – 'To the best mum in the world'.

These interludes were her last positive days; she had indeed lost weight, and by now was thrilled that her 5' 8" frame comfortably fit into a size 10.

At this time Caitlin met a new circle of non-college friends, including a boyfriend called Steven. She neglected her long-time friends at college, and out of the blue she began bunking off college in spite of the fact that she had rehearsals for a solo in the term-time cabaret. An interview at her first choice of university awaited. Dear Uncle Roy from America had promised to buy her an old banger of a car and, icing on the cake, she had a lovely summer job waiting for her in the south of France with a family and children she knew and loved. But on her last Thursday she didn't come home from college. Later she rang to say she would be spending the night with one of her new friends, Kathy, and would catch the bus to college from Kathy's on Friday morning. Might she bring Steven home for a meal Friday evening, as he'd like to meet me? Yes, of course, said I, we'll cook the meal together.

I discovered that Caitlin didn't go in to college when her tutor rang on Friday morning asking where she was. I rang Kathy's house.

'Caitlin, what's going on? You promised you were going to college. They need you for rehearsals.'

'Get off my case, Mum.' And then, as if she were playing a part in one of those 'because I'm worth it' ads, she shouted, 'I'm confident, I'm intelligent and I'm beautiful.' I was stunned.

'Caitlin, your personal excellence is not the issue here. Please come home, we are supposed to be cooking a meal for you and Steven.'

'He's not well, he's in bed with flu.'

'*Please* come home. What about your doctor's appointment?' At this point I was grasping at straws.

'Cancelled it. If you want me home, you'll have to come and get me.'

I refused. This person with Caitlin's voice was someone else entirely. She did not come home. Another first from a daughter who had always rung to let me know where she was, and another sleepless night for Mum on the home front, fretful, frustrated. And furious.

After it was too late to save Caitlin, I learned that she had gone pubbing on the Thursday night with her acquaintances. The new boyfriend was shift working at the local factory and Caitlin gathered every daffodil from an adjacent lay-by. She found Steven's office and showered the flowers at his feet, declaring her undying love. Then she walked back to Kathy's for the night. Next morning while chatting to Kathy, she calmly cut a neat 'S' on the back of her left hand, then rubbed a burn mark from the base of her forefinger to her wrist with a pencil rubber. She asked if Kathy wanted to try this: 'It doesn't hurt while you're doing it – it takes five minutes to hurt,' she said. Kathy declined, and later told me that Caitlin was being very 'mechanical and strange' that morning.

Nor did Caitlin come home on the Saturday. I phoned Kathy's at noon and Caitlin had just left. Through the afternoon I hovered round the phone waiting for her to contact me.

The phone rang at about 5 p.m. A female voice on the line:

'Is this Caitlin's mother?' Yes. 'Come and collect your daughter.'

'Who is this please?'

'Someone who thought Caitlin was a friend, but she's not, she's horrid.'

'Excuse me?'

'She's been beastly to our friend Steven. He really loves her, but she got off with Bristol Bob in the girls' cubicle at the Barley Mow. We told the publican and Caitlin's out on her arse.'

'I'm on my way.'

I drove the 15-mile journey like a maniac. Pulling up at the village's T-junction, a tableau from hell – Caitlin, struggling to free herself from a small gang of girls who were restraining her arms, pulling her hair. The shop window behind them, broken. A bearded shopkeeper wearily sweeping up the shards of glass. I spoke first to him.

'I'm so sorry, who broke your window? Have you phoned the police?'

The man wearily glanced up. 'We don't phone the police round here.'

How could this be my Caitlin, my daughter, broken and bleeding and flailing around like a snared wild bird, having kicked in a shop window? A bare 10 yards down the road a straggle of lads restrained Steven, the new boyfriend, pinning him to the spot. At first Caitlin didn't seem to recognize me – 'How did you know where I was?' she barked. She refused to get in our car until I suggested we invite Steven home with us to sort out whatever the problem was. Extracting him from the other group, I helped them into the car and drove them back home. Caitlin was simultaneously incoherent with remorse and alarmingly 'high'. I offered to cook them something.

Caitlin wanted to do the cooking. Did they want time alone to sort things out? Yes.

'I'll be back in an hour. I'm with Trish at Richard's and Lisa's if you need me. Don't drink any more alcohol. Promise?'

'Promise.'

On my return, Caitlin, standing jacketed in the front room, said that they weren't staying because our house gave Steven the creeps. She'd rung a taxi, and they were going out. Where? Anywhere but here! Caitlin seemed furious with me; her aggression was palpable. I watched helplessly as the taxi took them away. Another sleepless night.

Sunday morning. I rang Steven's home. Steven's mother answered the phone. Yes, Caitlin was there, and awake. What a lovely daughter you have. She's welcome to stay with us any time. Caitlin came to the phone.

'Darling, do you want to come home?'

'Yes, but Mum, I thought you were angry with me.'

I took a deep stupefied breath. 'Don't worry. See you in a few minutes.'

Most alarming to me at that point was the mutilation of her hand; she had never done anything like this, had always hated and avoided any sort of physical pain. She'd tried and failed at the current fashions of nose and belly button studs and piercing. I asked if she'd like to see the doctor. Yes.

Dr Lambert, who had prescribed Prozac for Caitlin, met us at the surgery and tended Caitlin's wounds. She asked Caitlin to tell her what had happened the day before. Did Caitlin think her medication might be a problem? Caitlin said maybe. Caitlin should see a psychiatrist as soon as possible, said Dr Lambert. Caitlin said yes please. Arm in arm we walked home in the Sunday sunshine; this has become a precious memory. Caitlin seemed at peace, serene. Never, never, in her life, she said, had she been so out of control as she was on Saturday. Did I think Steven would finish with her? Not if he's a proper new penny, I said. I told her that I loved her more than everything in the world but that I was running out of ideas. 'So am I, Mum.' Thinking that alcohol was the problem and that she just couldn't keep up with her friends' drinking habits, Caitlin planned to stop.

She went to bed for a while, exhausted, and in the afternoon spent time with Steven, trying to reassure him and make things up. At no point did I consider the possibility that her medication was the problem. I didn't know then what I know now, that this type of drug, taken by countless millions as a safe and non-addictive treatment for depression, changes the chemical constituency of the brain, and that approximately 10 per cent of the population do not possess the enzyme to metabolize it, leading in these people to a potentially toxic build-up.

On Monday Caitlin went to college. I kissed her goodbye at 6 a.m. and dashed off to catch my train to work. At some point she wrote and posted a card to Steven, declaring her desire to be '110% for you'. She apologized profusely for being 'more out of control than I've ever been. I promise I'll put my nutty behaviour in the past and sort out my head', she wrote. I last heard Caitlin's voice when I phoned from work that evening to tell her my train arrival time. She sounded cheerful, said that it had been a 'good news day', and asked me to listen to her solo song when I got home. 'Love you, Mum.'

Later records confirm that she phoned Steven at an agreed time; that he heard the phone ringing, but didn't answer it because he was discussing with his parents a pay rise he'd just received. He also didn't answer, as he explained at the inquest, because he knew it was Caitlin ringing at a prearranged time and was uncertain about his feelings for her. Between the time of Caitlin's attempt to ring him and his return call, she took her piano stool and stacked a childhood chair on top of it, made a ligature from her pony's lunge rope, slung it three times round a beam in the guest bedroom and twice tightly round her neck, placed a pillowcase over her head, and kicked away her support. She was still warm when we brought her down and attempted to resuscitate her. The postmortem reported only the presence of 'a therapeutic dose' in her system of 'fluoxetine hydrochloride (Prozac)', the drug she had been prescribed.

Caitlin left two notes, one carved on the collar of her lurcher dog, Gus: 'I love you, Gus, always'.

And one to me:

Mum,
I am so very sorry. I love you very much, and I always will. When you look at the stars, think of me smiling down at you, and Dad, and Sean and all of my friends and the people I care about. I am sorry I am a complete failure and a coward. I finally thought my life was going well and now everyone hates me. Remember me always and the good things I did instead of the bad. One day I

will meet you all again in heaven, if there is such a place. There are so many people I love that it would take a very long time for me to write them all. Remind people that I was a kind girl who loved to make people smile, so people don't remember all the bad things about me. I'm so very, very sorry. I love you with all of my heart. With you in spirit always

    All My Love Eternally,
     Caitlin

There's a mother in this scenario and she's me. I have longed for madness, but an incurable sanity afflicts me. The need to discover a 'Why?', leaving no stone unturned. I am informed that this is a near-universal response of grieving parents, and especially in cases of suicide or murder, and that 'letting go', 'moving on', 'finding closure' are mandatory. Some may say that Caitlin was suffering from undiagnosed depression – that is, 'the disease was responsible for her death, not the drug'; more cynical observers might feel that her death while on a drug that makes so many people feel great was coincidental. Still others who accept the connection between her suicide and the medication may see her death as collateral damage (acceptable failure) in the fight against depression – 'you win some, you lose some'. Clearly, I believe I know 'why', but knowing why changes nothing. And I'm sorry to say that it doesn't help either, because all I could ever want is my beloved girl alive.

What *does* help has become the 'stuff' of this book. Reaching out to parents, grandparents, sisters, brothers, adopted or blood-related, who have lost a child, or an only child – or, in some cases, children – and who, in spite of intimate acquaintance with sorrow, take courage to re-build from the ruins and carry on with life. Nobody wants to think that you have to suffer in order to grow. Would it were not so, and I'm certain that suffering is not the only motor of growth. But suffering can be forged into a 'terrible beauty'. I may not like it, but I've seen it too many times to discount it.

My earlier life projects in teaching, publishing and broadcasting have involved thousands of students and participants, many of whom I know only through correspondence, but who have enriched both work and life beyond measure. All researchers are taught that scientific objectivity depends on keeping one's distance from the people one writes about, but, for me, grief, the great leveller, changes all that. I am persuaded that writing from a 'befriending' perspective will be helpful, not least by serving as an important reminder that all human 'objects' are primarily 'subjects', that this book will be enriched by first-hand experience as well as more traditional methodologies. As Caitlin wrote in her diary, 'A friend is the one who comes in when the world has gone out.'

After 11 September 2001, New York Christians hosted one of many services for British families who lost loved ones. Prime Minister Tony Blair attended, and contributed a reading. He chose a passage from Thornton Wilder's *The Bridge of San Luis Rey*. In this novella, the finest bridge in all of Peru broke, killing five people in the midst of living the story of their lives. The author writes of their lives up to the time they are about to set off across the bridge. Tony Blair read out the last paragraph:

> . . . soon . . . all memory of those five will have left the earth, and we ourselves shall be loved for a while and forgotten. But the love will have been enough; all those impulses of love return to the love that made them. Even memory is not necessary for love. There is a land . . . of the living and a land of the dead, and the bridge is love, the only survival, the only meaning.

Grief is many things; it is a place, here where I stand, and a feeling, and also an objective experience; but perhaps most accurately it is an architect of restoration and renewal to the ruined bridge of loss. It is physically and mentally painful, sometimes to an indescribable degree. We all want to avoid it, but there are times when we cannot. We grow up. We grow older. Some of us even grow wiser. I am not certain that we can ever *choose* to grow a 'good grief', but, frankly, it is worth a try.

Who is this book for?

This is a befriending book for the mothers, fathers, siblings and grandparents bereaved of their child or children, and, in the words of the tagline for The Compassionate Friends, 'for those similarly bereaved'. It will also be useful to friends who care about bereaved families as well as to helping agencies. The category 'child' includes adult offspring as well as 'chronological children', and grandparents bereaved of grown children or grandchildren.

Most of us feel inadequate in the face of death. My purpose is to explore ways of healing and solace for those devastated by the anguish of grief, and to discover ways of offering comfort to friends and relatives to whom the unthinkable has happened.

This book addresses many, though not all, aspects of life after the death of a child. Perhaps most importantly it tackles the over-used, misunderstood and endlessly fascinating word 'love' that won't let us go, as well as the other two of the 'big three' graces, faith and hope. My hope for you is that this book may provide a brick or two for the building of an unbreakable bridge of love, hope and, for those who desire or perceive its importance, faith.

1
Growing Round Grief

> May the mountains stand to remind us
> Of what it means to be young.
> May we be outlived by our daughters.
> May we be outlived by our sons.

The above verse (Marsden, 1999) expresses the automatic hope or prayer of parents everywhere. When we welcome our children to the world, we know – if required to think about it – that we would give our lives for this growing person. However busy and fulfilling our adult lives and pursuits may be, our children are quite simply the delicious and exasperating today, our connection to tomorrow and to the broader community, the most important people in our lives, unique in every way. We want nothing less than the best for them.

A child born in 1998 can expect to the age of 79, some 29 years longer than a child born in 1900 (National (US) Center for Health Statistics, 2000). We privileged Westerners expect to be able to protect our children with good medical care, education and a supportive community in our affectionately described 'nanny' state. We presume that when we slip or fall short of ideal parenthood – and don't we all! – a community of co-ordinated professional wisdom will, if necessary, be at our disposal and come to the rescue. It's not that we are immune to suffering; daily we hear desperate stories of lost, disappeared or murdered children, even of places on the planet where children are hunted and disposed of like social vermin. We sympathize, we tut-tut – we may even shed tears. Yet always it seems that such disaster happens to others. Indeed, I believe that we should be grateful for this protective buffer zone of exemption, this layer of 'it only happens to others'. Why? Because it allows us to be brave on our own and our child's behalf without being overwhelmed by fear. It allows us the comfort of believing that we are special, protected, cared for, and in some cases it gives us the strength to reach out in solidarity, trying to make a difference. It allows us to construct meaning in our existence and that of our child.

It is, however, an uncomfortable fact that the death of our children is not a rarity. Far from it. Accidents, incurable illness, stillbirths, suicides, disasters and murders claim the lives of children on a regular basis in the 'developed' world, and in the developing world in epidemic proportions. Whether expected or not, sudden, preventable or 'natural', death happens 'out of joint' to the young in our society. In England and Wales, in 2001, more than 5,000 children died before reaching their first birthday. Fewer died between the ages of one and 14, but figures rise dramatically for those who died before their fifteenth birthday. Extending the age to 24 brings the total figure close to 8,000, and by age 34, to more than 13,000 offspring who died (Office of National Statistics, 2002). However, the fact remains that the death of one's child, or children, remains the worst thing that can happen, one of life's unfathomable tragedies. We cry with the bereaved parent, 'To the world she was one child, to me she was the world' and 'This is the wrong way round!'

But death is 'common', not only in that it happens eventually to all of us – one of life's few certainties – but that it happens to *our* children. I place the word 'common' in inverted commas because I discussed it in some detail with my editor and with many friends in the course of writing the book. A flagship list of Sheldon Press is the impressive and popular 'overcoming *common* problems' series. This set me to thinking about the things we call 'common'. 'Common' is 'not unusual'. It is ordinary, regular. 'Common' belongs to the public, as in 'common ground' and 'common knowledge'; or 'common', being land owned by a town and open to the use of all. Sometimes it is used to denote coarseness, vulgarity, or 'low lifers', as in 'common thief'. In England it means 'not of the upper classes', and most of us are 'commoners'. Common dolphins, sparrows, places where people gather – we speak positively about 'common sense', the 'common good'. And so on. Perhaps that which is common is more important than that which is unique – or, if not more important, at least *as* important.

I remember a favourite teacher once quipping that for the Victorians, sex was taboo and death an obsession, while to our culture the opposite is the case: death being taboo and sex an obsession. It is certainly the case that Western society, deprived of a unified belief system, tends to push a proper understanding of mortality into the background. Sometimes attitudes towards death conspire unwittingly to increase feelings of isolation and uniqueness. This can even be the case with helping agencies and communities whose remit is helping bereaved parents and siblings. It is easy to forget that cultural meanings are central to the impact of death on close relatives, and any supporting agency would do well to gain knowledge of each family's complex beliefs and conventions of mourning. For close members of grieving families this seems an obvious observation, but it is surprisingly often overlooked by helping agencies and well-meaning friends alike. To put it more simply, thinking about death is important and, more to the point, *what* we think about death is important (see Chapter 2). Moreover, what others understand about what we think is equally important.

If asked to describe our most commonly felt experiences in the wake of losing a child, bereaved parents will quite likely say a version of one or two things: 'I feel so alone, so isolated in my grief,' or, 'Nobody understands what I'm going through, not my own family, the counsellors or police or bereavement specialists – nobody.' We also may say, 'To be honest, I don't want you even to *say* you understand; and please, please don't ask me how I am, because you won't really want to hear!'

This is an important issue. Most bereaved parents would not wish anyone else to be required to experience the particular desolation of a child's death. I say 'most', because there are exceptions – for example, in cases of violent death and murder, where revenge may be a strong and understandable motivator. But most parents crushed by a child's death would simply hope for empathy and understanding. The isolation of bereaved parents and surviving siblings serves as a talisman to implore that this horror does not occur to one's fellow human beings. Yet in our heart of hearts we know that such power is not within our reach, that this darkness will happen again – it will happen with no respect of persons to the good, the beautiful, the bad, the ugly. Is it even possible to prepare for the unthinkable? And can one heal the unbearable? Is it possible to be together in our aloneness?

Joe and Iris Lawley, co-founders of The Compassionate Friends (see Chapter 7), lost their 12-year-old son Kenneth in a road traffic accident (Mirren, 1995):

> You soon learn that no one really understands, except those who have also lost a child. Please, please don't let one other kind person say to me 'I understand' is the commonest outcry from those who have lost a child. Comments such as 'I know how you

feel, I lost my granny, my poodle, etc.' stretch you to breaking point. I'm sure we said the same kind of things before we lost Kenneth, but even though you know people are just trying to be kind and helpful, you are so sensitive and vulnerable that any claim of another person to 'know how you feel' is seen as an attempt to link some suffering of theirs with your shattered existence. The comparisons offered, we know, are simply meant as some bridge by which they can reach us, but sadly the words used create the barrier.

The Lawleys' observations find an echo in the lives of countless bereaved parents; there are apparently no generally applicable palliatives for parental and sibling grief. When Caitlin died I did receive some messages of crass and breathtaking insensitivity. One friend rang to say how beautiful the funeral was, and wound the conversation up by saying how good it was that such throngs came to 'make up numbers' in our large country parish church. This unleashed a fury in me that caught me totally unawares. True, the church was overflowing; we live in a tiny community and we have no secrets. Caitlin's death was a community tragedy and numbers at the funeral reflected this. I was more than aware that, had she died in London, the funeral might well have been small, reflecting the anonymity of city life and, too often, of death.

Another friend took hold of me in the local post office, begged me to give her a hug, and said that she had recently gone through the similar loss when she had to have her horse put down. This is not to underplay the depth of love one has for a horse, pony, poodle or pet, but to make such a comparison is invidious and often damaging in these circumstances. You may say that I am stating the obvious. You are correct.

Still, on one level I found the Lawleys' observation personally disturbing. In a lifetime of teaching and writing, as mother of two children and a Christian by persuasion, I have carried a conscious commitment to understanding 'history' *without* having to repeat it, while at the same time empathizing with those who have gone through the experience firsthand. A body of great literature presents us with endless examples of vicarious knowledge. One needn't commit genocide or murder in order to explore a murderer's mind, become a mercenary or terrorist or felon to reach into the mental workings of a war veteran or thief. In fictional forays I take huge pleasure in imagining what it is like to be someone else, wearing their shoes even if they pinch, and then writing their story. Understanding without experiencing, without judging, I thought and taught, comes from the very heart of educating oneself, listening to and watching those who leave their stories for us to absorb and to learn from ... write about what you know by learning from what you write.

Then the intimate thunderbolt of Caitlin's death by suicide struck. Suddenly here I was, feeling for the first time a truly Dark Night of the Soul, a total defeat of everything I stood for. ('Therefore choose life!' was the very stuff and mainstay of my work and vocation, and yet my beloved daughter appeared to have chosen death.) I was alone, unable to communicate the unimaginable, entirely diminished, a dancing shadow without my dancer. And, admittedly, not sure that I *wanted* to be understood by those who were trying to support me. I truly didn't want anyone to feel what I was feeling and, to be honest, I still don't. To apprehend, to empathize, yes, but protected, to use the Apostle Paul's phrase, seeing 'through a glass darkly', by which I mean a kind of virtual reality experience, a reflection and not the thing itself – not 'face to face'.

Sisters and brothers share with parents and grandparents these feelings of isolation and invisibility (see Chapter 4). Surviving siblings all too often experience exclusion, guilt and resentment, along with unexplained tuggings of grief ... a sense of unique isolation in spite of being surrounded by family and friends. Many sisters and brothers cannot speak to anyone about their deepest emotions after the death of their sibling, believing, as one correspondent stated, 'What's the point? *Nobody* understands how I feel.' Often siblings have viewed their brother or sister as a rival, which can leave them feeling very guilty. Older brothers and sisters feel they need to protect parents, which includes protecting Mum and Dad from their own pain. People ask, 'How are they doing?' – 'they' usually being Mum and/or Dad – and apparently seldom ask, 'How are *you*?'

Our individualist-oriented society too often exacerbates this isolation. Grief tends to be placed squarely on the shoulders of the bereaved individual, and in single-parent, adoptive and stepfamilies the problem is too frequently compounded. Nearly half the children in England and Wales are not being brought up in a 'traditional' family – that is, with parents married and living together under the same roof (Office for National Statistics, 2003). Counsellors often continue to emphasize that on a one-to-one basis, the bereaved parent or sibling has an individual 'problem' to solve, 'grief work' to complete, a good deal of 'letting go', 'moving on' and that dreary word 'closure' to complete. These techniques may not always be helpful and instead increase the experience of isolation. In her poem 'Grief', Lin Baldwin – who lost her 16-year-old son, Tom, suddenly – wrestles away on her own as the world sleeps:

> I meet the cruelty of grief in the night
> It holds me in its metal claws
> Ravages me with iron jaws
> Tosses me from side to side
> Ripping and rending deep inside
>
> And it won't let go
> Oh no
> Oh no
> It is a relentless beast
> Implacable in its torture
> But it won't kill
> Oh no
> Oh no
>
> The sport is too fine
> For I am a tough little morsel
> The better to crack
> Plenty of love
> And no lack of marrow in memories
> A lifetime of laughter and joy to sack
>
> So it stretches me out upon the rack
> Of the certain knowledge
> That he won't come back

Isolation has not always been the case. Without romanticizing the past, it is accepted by many students of history that earlier cultures, in which the death of children was more frequent, tended to place death at the centre of a community life bolstered by commonly held belief systems which we often mistakenly mock without understanding. In these communities there would be agreement about how the event could be worked through, so that when a child died (and it is important to point out that the anguish was no less than ours) there would be a collective mourning, carrying the important function of honouring the death within an environment of shared grieving and memories, layered by rituals and domestic structures to allow continuing bonds with the dead person.

In the wake of my daughter's death I clung like a limpet to expert listening ears – my own GP and personal friend, two CRUSE counsellors, my spiritual director, as well as the loving and patient friends who held me in all the mess. In spite of this extensive support, I felt totally alone in doing a great deal of 'grief work'. I wanted them to accept my fervent and half-shamed admission that I would rather Caitlin were alive even if she were totally paralysed and brain-impaired. My 'reasoning', such as it was, was this: there would still be a breathing someone who looked like Caitlin to care for. The responses to this cry from the heart was pretty consistent: 'Don't be so selfish.' Or, more gently, 'It's early days, Linda. You'll change.' Was this extreme thought on my part a pathological expression of grief? Or would it quite simply be a longing for an impossible bargain with death?

Findings regarding stages of bereavement, the need to complete metaphorical 'grief packages', appear to have limited value in helping many bereaved parents. I am persuaded that the brilliant Elisabeth Kübler-Ross never envisaged a shrine being erected over her 'stages of grief'. Again and again, parents and siblings who have lost their loved ones beg listeners to avoid terms that they perceive to be condescending or insulting to the memory of the child, terms that simply do not fit any preconceived plot – for example, 'coming to terms', 'finding closure', 'letting go', 'moving on', 'not your fault', 'it was her/his choice' (in cases of suicide), 'getting on with life', 'getting angry', 'getting over it', 'recovering'.

This is not mere belligerence. Catharine and Michael Pointer were leaving church with their children Rachel and Jonathan on a Harvest Festival Sunday in 1983. Their lives were changed for ever when a driver approached them at speed, cut across their path and mounted the pavement, taking the Pointers with him. Michael and Rachel suffered chest and head injuries; their son Jonathan was less badly injured. Catharine's injuries were spinal. Michael survived his serious injuries, but little Rachel, nearly seven, did not survive the accident, and her mother was paralysed. Catharine observed that the medical staff treated the case of paralysis, but unwittingly neglected the grieving mother, as attested in Ena Mirren's anthology *Our Children* (1995):

> Apart from Rachel's paediatrician ... and the humane and humorous GP to whom we later changed, the medical profession seemed strangely at a loss in offering us any help in the early stages. However helpful professional theories about bereavement may be to those seeking to help, the greatest support may come from *someone simply being there, listening and taking an interest and not being afraid to ask about the child who has died* [my italics].

Being there. Listening. Taking an interest. Not being afraid to talk about our child. A background in biblical scholarship leads me to certain iconic bereaved parents – King David; Job; Mary, the mother of Jesus. How I wish the authors told us whether King David 'moved on' after the sudden death of his wild and rebellious son Absalom, of whose death he cried, 'O Absalom, my son, my son, would God I had died for you. O Absalom, my son.' How did Job 'achieve closure' in his new family after the testing by Satan and subsequent loss of *all* possessions and *all* his dozen children? His friends chastised him for being 'depressed', though of course they didn't use the term – Job's wife survived; she'd counselled Job to throw in the towel, to 'curse God and die' when Job was covered in suppurating boils and in the depths of his grief.

And Jesus' mother, Mary? Not long after Caitlin's death I experienced what I can only describe as a fundamental kinship with Mary; I dreamed that she feared her son was, through his actions, virtually acceding to suicide but that she was helpless to stop him. How, I mused, could Mary bear to witness her son's conscious path to torture and death after being stitched up by one of his closest friends and by the religious leaders of his own faith, *her* faith, the faith his family had been taught to respect from time immemorial? How must Mary have felt when, from the cross, Jesus pointed to the beloved disciple John and said to his mother, shivering helplessly at the foot of his cross, 'Woman, behold your son'? Would she say, 'Good idea, Son, *your* choice, I'm letting go now'?

It is not fair to impose certain twenty-first-century notions on events that occurred two millennia earlier. Resignation – 'Thy will be done' – was perhaps more deeply implanted in biblical days, in contrast to our current cultural rages 'against the dying of the light'. It is, however, fair to say that bereavement is a constant of human history, as are responses to it. It is not that our concepts are ill-intentioned. People who love us grievers want us to get better! And if grief were a disease, this might be eminently sensible. It is just quite simply a fact that those who counsel to 'pull up one's socks', or absolve one from all connection to the loss, to opine that one is an 'innocent victim', too often bypass the expressed and central needs of the grieving parent and intimate loved ones.

It may be necessary, for example, to recognize that there is such a thing as being inconsolable, and that this hugely difficult state arises from a brute fact – the death of a unique and irreplaceable human being. Indeed, for some parents, the meaning of life vanishes with the loss of their child, and grief comes to provide the new 'meaning' . . . not requested, but inflicted by desolation, for a time at least. Shakespeare recognized this:

> Grief fills the room up of my absent child,
> Lies in his bed, walks up and down with me,
> Puts on his pretty looks, repeats his words,
> Remembers me of all his gracious parts,
> Stuffs out his vacant garments with his form;
> Then have I reason to be fond of grief.
>
> (*King John*, IV, l, 93)

Of all the stories on my author's dream list, this book is one I would never have wanted to write. When Caitlin was alive I'd published two works of non-fiction, completed two novels, and was working furiously on a third. After her death nothing seemed to matter, the bleak mantra of Ecclesiastes echoing in the brain – 'vanity vanity, sayeth the preacher, all is vanity'. It was as if one event, and one event only, had happened.

I soon found that I needed to confront a tangled part of myself. It was the part of me denying that *being* rather than *imagining being* a bereaved parent would help write a *better* book. I've spent a lot of energy in this life pretending that any personal misfortune was not really 'personal', because I was 'different'. Like the saints I loved reading about as a child, like my cult heroes Martin Luther King and

Mahatma Gandhi and my mother Rosalie, I had been to the mountaintop and seen the promised land. I 'had the dream' too, of making a difference in the world. Heady stuff, and I think in my case, with hindsight, this is called denial. Self-examination brought disturbing discoveries – for example, I realized that I have personally lived through most of the kinds of bereavement explored in these pages, plus the death of my mother Rosalie to Hodgkin's disease when I was six years old. After much contorted analysis I came to the conclusion that I was, after all, not so different; moreover, being a woman 'of sorrow and acquainted with grief' would go some way towards making this a better book – something that others probably knew without a second thought.

Having spoken in such candid personal terms, I pay tribute to the research and wisdom gleaned from the generous body of dedicated studies of bereavement that inform these pages. My purpose is to present the best of what has been learned from the psychology of child bereavement, as well as extensive use of the words and experiences of people who are living through the loss of a child or children of all ages, discovering ways of remembering without becoming stuck, of honouring without bathos.

On the road has come inspiration from many fronts – from concerned experts worldwide who offer support to one another, and importantly from The Compassionate Friends, an international organization whose UK quarterly journal I edit. These are people who know the importance of both peer support and social connectedness. There is a debt of gratitude, too, to Jean Taylor, the CRUSE counsellor who pointed me to the following story.

Many books written about bereavement suggest that people go through various stages in working through their grief, and that in the end the grief gets resolved, or the 'grief work' finished. However, this is not everyone's experience. Some people find that the pain never really seems to go away completely and is sometimes as bad as it ever was. Here is another way of looking at grief that might make sense. It comes from an article by Lois Tonkin, a grief counsellor in New Zealand, and first published in the CRUSE publication *Bereavement Care* (Tonkin, 1997); it is based on a conversation between the author and a woman whose child had died several years earlier. When the woman's child died, the bereaved mother found that her grief consumed her totally; she drew a circle to illustrate this:

Figure 1

The circle represents her life; the dark shading is her grief. She imagined, and in fact had been told repeatedly, that in time the grief would shrink and become a small but manageable part of her life:

Figure 2

What happened, though, was completely different. The woman's grief stayed just as large as ever, but her life grew round her grief:

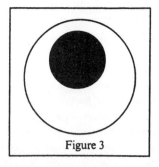

Figure 3

There were times – anniversaries and other bad moments that reminded her of her child – when her sadness was as intense as ever and she was operating entirely from the shaded circle on the diagram. But increasingly she found she was experiencing life in the larger circle.

This concept of grief won't apply to everyone who is bereaved, but those who can relate to it may find it comforting. It stops us worrying why the grief isn't becoming less, explains the dark days, and describes how our life has expanded through the profound experience of grief. It means we can grow without feeling any sense of disloyalty to the person we have lost. It's a process of integrating the loss with our lives so as to manage to continue life after the death of our loved one.

The model outlined above is just one pattern of living after the loss of a child. Think of it as a touchstone for the rest of the book. Here are some assumptions we will examine:

- The assumption that death irrevocably severs the relationship between the living and the dead.
- The assumption that 'letting go' is necessary. Therapies that encourage detachment from the deceased may not always be helpful.
- Conversely, the assumption that avoiding grief is unhealthy may be misplaced. Individuals who fail to express deep distress after bereavement may not be postponing or suppressing it, and therapies that encourage some bereaved people to face painful feelings may not always be appropriate.
- The assumption that the best way of 'holding on' is 'letting go'.
- The assumption that bereavement can happen in isolation from family and social networks.
- The assumption that time heals all wounds. When a much-loved person dies, this is often perceived as a near-mortal wound or an amputation. However, more than this, the death leads to a changed relationship. We long for the old one, but this is not possible. We miss this child in an unending way. We want them to know that this is how we feel.

Bereavement is like the proverbial pebble dropped in the pool, creating endless ripples. For some it is an ocean of permanent turbulence. It affects not only individual members of a family, but will also directly affect the ways in which the surviving members relate to one another. It places great strains on the family. Communication patterns and roles will change as a result of each member's perceptions of the grief of the others, and of their own feeling of inclusion or exclusion from the death.

Openness or censure over the expression of feelings, permission or restriction of conversations about the deceased arising from the grief responses of any one family member, may set the tone for all communication relating to the bereavement, and affect the degree to which the family can operate as a resource for, or as an obstacle to, rebuilding life. Each family member will be additionally influenced by relationships external to the family. These relationships may affect assumptions regarding responsibility for other members and the degree to which they need or desire to explore their own feelings within the family.

The pattern of our grief is as unique as our fingerprints, shaped by our very specific life circumstances and unique personalities. But as surely as our fingerprint is on a finger that is on a hand that reaches out to hold and clasp the similar hand of our friends, the patterns of grief also connect to an intricate, interconnected web of community. Comforters and friends may be unable to tell grieving partners and friends *how* to feel, but they may be able to help discover ways to affirm and to continue living, to evolve new meanings when the old ones are gone for ever. To journey through grieving, and to grow around it.

2

Early Days: When We're Not Strong

10.28 p.m., 3.25 a.m., 12 noon . . . our child has just died. We will remember the precise time we hear this devastating news, and we will definitely not forget the day. We have just gone through the most catastrophic event of our life. The world is changed for ever and the new one isn't looking either recognizable or inviting.

It is 10.28 p.m., 6 April 1998, the Monday of Holy Week, and my train pulls in promptly to the home station. It's been a long day which began at 5 a.m., working in London, some four hours' journey away. My partner Trish is waiting for me with Caitlin's dog, Gus. I notice that he isn't wearing his collar – 'Gus is naked!' I joke, and Trish says that Caitlin had probably removed it. We chat and relax during the 15-minute drive from station to home.

'How was Caitlin today?' I ask.

'Lots of phone calls and chats with Amy – seems subdued, but OK,' says Trish.

'Phew! She was sound as a pound on the phone when I rang her from the office . . . and after the weekend from hell!'

Arriving home we were greeted by the Oasis album *Be Here Now* at full blast, a CD I'd bought for Caitlin a few weeks previously. I rushed to the living room, turned down the volume, and called her name. No reply. I called a second time, 'Cakes!' When there was no answer I trotted upstairs and saw that her bedroom door was open, the light on. I trundled back down to the kitchen, mumbling that she must have popped over to see Amy across the road. Trish said this was quite likely as Caitlin had been looking for my tape recorder earlier to practise and listen to the playback of the song she'd be singing in performance next day (Simply Red's 'If you don't know me by now'), and had gone over to Amy's earlier.

I poured myself a cider, slid a chunk of cheese between two slabs of bread, and quite suddenly didn't feel like either eating or drinking. We moved up to the lounge, waiting for Caitlin's return; it was nearly 11 p.m. – she couldn't be far.

Suddenly, Trish got up and said, 'I'm going to find Gus's collar before I forget.' Within seconds she brought the collar down and was putting it back on Gus's neck. She said, 'Caitlin's carved a note on . . .' She didn't finish the sentence and ran back upstairs.

Simultaneously, the phone rang. It was Caitlin's new boyfriend, Steven. 'Is Caitlin there?'

I'd not yet answered him, when Trish screamed from upstairs, 'Linda! Come up now – no, *don't* come up! Caitlin's—'

'Something's wrong,' I told Steven. 'I've got to go now,' I said, put the phone down, and bolted upstairs.

Caitlin was hanging from a beam in the guest bedroom. Trish was trying to bring her down. I embraced my daughter around her thighs and lifted with all my strength to help Trish release her from the ligature. Caitlin felt light. She was still warm. We placed her on the bed and removed the pillowcase from her head. Although she was cyanosed, to me she did not look dead. Trish, an experienced first-aider, began cardio-pulmonary resuscitation immediately, and I flew downstairs to phone our doctor. Dr Gray arrived within ten minutes to attend to Caitlin. Minutes later she appeared in the study where I stood frozen to the spot.

'We couldn't save her.' Dr Gray declared Caitlin dead at 11.30 p.m. I lay down beside Caitlin, and Trish covered us with a duvet. The police arrived. I gave a statement. A scenes-of-crime officer took 12 photographs, the last photographs of my beloved girl. He was crying. And then the ambulance came and took her body away for the postmortem necessary when the circumstances of death are suspicious. I did not want to be prevented from accompanying her body. I wanted to attend and to witness everything these strangers did to her, but this was not permitted. At midnight I rang my beloved friend, neighbour and priest, Graham Dowell, to tell him Caitlin had hanged herself. He came and prayed with me. I cannot recall if they had already taken Caitlin's body away at this point, and dear Graham has since died and so I cannot ask him.

Caitlin's death on that night has a sound, a touch and a colour. The sound is a flatline hum, like a drilling into the brain, a sound that seemed to me to begin when Caitlin's spirit or life essence could not get back into her body. If evil has a sound, it was this sound. If it has a sense of touch, it is a prickly sickly highly alert frisson of horror like an electric shock to the soul. The colour of her death is a dull yellow.

Charlie Walton, who with his wife Kay (then his girlfriend) were friends of mine back in university days, lost two sons, Tim and Don, in 1986. Bryan, the boys' friend and only son of their best friends, also died in what appears to have been a youthful experiment gone horribly and tragically wrong. In his book called *When There Are No Words* (Walton, 1996) Charlie writes:

> From the very first instant of the officer's clumsy announcement of our sons' deaths, my mind processes information calmly . . . too calmly. I understand. I comprehend. I hate it . . . but I think through the implications and alternatives. My mind never goes blank. It doesn't even shut down temporarily as I might have expected. I long to lose control . . . freak out . . . scream . . . faint. Those seem like the appropriate responses . . . the natural human responses that I would write if I were scripting this scene for television. But those responses are not my nature. One of the standing jokes in our family is that 'Dad is always calm and controlled in emergencies – it's daily life that makes him fall apart!'
>
> I process immediately the fact that our baby and the comedian who often introduced himself as 'the middle child' are both dead. I am never going to see them again . . . alive in their familiar bodies. To this day, I have not yet processed the fact that Bryan died with them. Bryan . . . the only son of our close friends . . . with whom we had shared good times and bad. Kay says, 'I think I'm going to be sick.'

Charlie and Kay held things together as best they could and, with the help of friends who gathered round immediately, made it through what was left of that night.

Guilt, whys, what-ifferies and if onlys

These will be very close at hand if we feel we are in some way responsible for our child's death. Were we neglectful, too casual, too over-protective, too trusting, too impatient, too exhausted, too set in our ways? Could we have done anything more? Should we have been more loving? Less strict? More gentle? And the 'whys':

- Why didn't I listen when she said she might as well be dead?
- Why did I secretly say, one day when at the end of my tether, that I hated him when he behaved so hurtfully?
- Why didn't I spend more time with her?

- Why did I criticize his father/mother after the divorce?
- Why didn't I spend more time playing, discussing, trusting?
- Why is this list of 'whys' so seemingly endless?

In the period immediately following our bereavement, we will quite likely find that our sleep is disturbed and feel incredible fatigue, forever exhausted. Medication and/or alcohol, though, will exacerbate rather than ease these responses. Feelings of guilt can be overpowering – and sometimes may even be appropriate if they lead somewhere positive. It may, for example, be the case that we were implicated, and we feel we may never be able to forgive ourselves unless we go through the painful possibility of our culpability. An example from a recently bereaved acquaintance is of death following an unfinished argument with the child. The child stormed out in a huff and tragically died – the last memory being of unresolved anger. This notion of taking responsibility is, I know, an unpopular one. We re-run the tape of 'what ifs' and 'if onlys' on an endless mental loop. When the loop pauses we may begin to perceive that whatever was missing, we did our very best. At that point guilt can begin a gradual return to self-forgiveness, reaping in an unfair world some release from the bondage of guilt.

As we choke on food, gaze at empty rooms and beds and chairs, shop for necessities and continue to purchase our child's favourite foods, as eventually we manage to live through the first anniversary of birthdays, holidays, with an absence – and we must – we fear that these feelings will never go away.

How to stop the pain? How to get out of bed today? How to remove that invisible nail holding our foot to the same spot? How to stop the tears, or the tearless ache? In crowds we are aware that nobody knows our world has changed for ever. Many bereaved parents long for a badge or ribbon, a mark of some kind, to identify our state. Our child is dead. 'Can people not see by looking at me that I have lost my child?' We are so alone, but we know the answer – that strangers cannot see our tragedy; that life goes on, and on.

Regrets

You may remember a song made famous by Frank Sinatra called 'My Way': 'Regrets, I've had a few, but then again too few to mention ...', or Edith Piaf's unforgettable anthem, *'Non! Rien de rien ... Non, je ne regrette rien!'* ('I regret nothing!')

As for me? I'm a regret bore. Regrets, like the poor, I have with me always. I jotted the following parody of 'My Way' in my journal:

> Regrets, I've got a lot,
> You must be very tired of hearing,
> At times I've lost the plot,
> A trait I know is not endearing . . .

Yet regret for the past is not only understandable, it is a sign of a life considered. Admitting regrets does not have the *hutzpah* of the Piafs and Sinatras of the world, but it's honest. And it does matter what we've done – or left undone – in our lives. The question is, what do we do with our regrets? The playwright Arthur Miller has one of his characters say, 'Maybe all one can do is hope to end up with the right regrets' – something to ponder.

Many grieving loved ones suffer physical as well as spiritual/ mental shatterings. My former husband Tom, an Anglican priest, became and remains seriously ill; Caitlin's brother Sean broke an ankle, dropped out of college, and suffered an incapacitating breakdown. In my case, friends said I was breathing oddly; secretly, I had taken to gathering poisonous seeds, mushrooms and berries from fields and hedgerows . . . just in case, just in case . . . but the physical body ticked away as healthily as any reasonably fit person of my age. People kept telling me how marvellous I looked and praising me for 'bearing up' so well, when truth told I couldn't discern the difference between being alive and being dead. The irony of it! It did make me smile, even early on.

Unusual thoughts

Margaret Bell's son Colan died in 1998, but at times the pangs of bereavement return as if it were yesterday. She writes in an issue of the *TCF Newsletter* (Bell, 2001):

My son's death was so sudden, no warning, no illness of any kind, that a postmortem had to be carried out to ascertain the cause of death. Why is it that I am now still so troubled, and cry for days on end, at the thought of a pathologist having to cut my lovely son from head to toe to look inside the body to which I

gave birth? Am I alone in thinking in this perhaps insane manner?
... When I saw Colan in the funeral parlour after 'all' was
completed, I dearly wanted to look inside the suit he had been
dressed in, but was deterred from doing so by well-meaning
relatives, and also the funeral director. I can understand the reason
– am I just being paranoid and what purpose would it serve even
if I had seen? This is just a wild thought in my mind, but you
never know, there may well be other tormented bereaved parents
who think along the same lines ... It seems that most of us have
similar thoughts at one time or another ... and it's good to know
that we are not entirely mad ... It takes time to absorb the
permanence of our loss, and the resulting reality of the complete
cessation of communication with our beloved child or children.
Storms pass and birds do sing again after a storm, and I do think
that humans can too – but isn't it so difficult? I feel weary and ill
at times and think that the storm will never cease, and to crown it
all my friends think that I should be 'over it'. Oh how I hate those
awful words ... Another little thing I did this summer was to
plant foxgloves in my garden ... lovely mixed colours. Why,
you may wonder? Well, when Colan was young and when I was
taking him to and from school ... on our way home we passed
through a lane which was often strewn with foxgloves. One day I
explained what I thought they represented, and I pulled off ten of
the 'gloves' and placed them on his thumbs and fingers. He was
so delighted with this simple gesture, and the procedure had to be
repeated each day until at last the foxgloves were no longer in
bloom. I shall never forget the love and wonderment in his eyes
as he looked up at me and said, 'Mum, you are my bestest love',
and I didn't even correct his grammar ... And now, these years
after his death, I have had foxgloves. I cried for days – why did I
put myself through this agony? Why do we do it? I suppose trying
to recapture what will never be ... for anyone out there who is
experiencing the same difficulty, don't worry about it – at times
like that I ask to be 'carried' and I know that I have been.

Parents whose children's organs have been retained without parental
permission will readily understand Margaret Bell's distress. It can
bring solace, though, to know that we are not alone in these
disconcerting thoughts.

When a child suffers a terminal illness we have, in some senses, time to prepare for our child's death, and may experience the tragedy of loss differently. In the following story, faith plays an important role. John Williams was a presenter for the BBC. His daughter Margaret, aged eight, was stricken with an inoperable brain tumour. In *On the Death of a Child* (Williams, 1965) he writes:

> On the day she died, a friend who was a Franciscan friar of the Church of England came to minister to her. He talked to her and prayed with her and gave her his blessing ... We don't know what he said or did – but I have never doubted that by some means he brought that child very near to God, and God very near to her; and her death, in spite of all the apparent waste and ugliness, was somehow *beautiful*. This is where it gets difficult to say ... but the astonishing calmness and courage and gentleness and patience of that child, as she came to the last big struggle and then slowly faded out, were remarkable to watch. Somehow that very ordinary, mischievous little girl seemed to have 'grown up' – she had become 'spiritual', if you know what I mean ...
>
> I felt I understood a bit more what the Transfiguration meant: the light shining through: the 'silver lining' ... One can't argue about things like that; you can only feel or sense them.
>
> It does raise a whole host of terrible problems and doubts, to watch a child slowly fade away and all her lovely gifts spoilt and wasted, and all over by the time she was eight years old. What a waste! Why does God let such things happen? Does he really care? ... I don't personally feel those doubts any longer. I don't believe it was God's purpose at all that all his lovely handiwork should be spoilt like that ... I am so sure that death (in whatever terrible forms it may come) is only an episode in life – a station where you change (if you like to put it so) and not the end of the journey, and that Margaret is still 'going on' without any of the handicaps of our limited bodily life. In some strange way, in spite of all that pain and loss, Margaret became a mature personality, spiritual and alive, and we still regard her as a member of the family and include her in our family prayers every night. Her life was *not* wasted ... 'a silver lining through the dark clouds shining' ....
>
> What you really believe about death is very important indeed, because death is the one and only thing about our future of which we can be absolutely certain. I can't be certain of anything else at

all. What I shall have for breakfast tomorrow ... surely the only sensible thing I can do about this fact is to 'come to terms' with the fact; think about it, try to understand what it means and where it is leading to, and then live the rest of my life accordingly. No one who has not come to terms with death has really to terms with anything ... If I believe that death is the end of everything worth living for, that all the things for which I fight and struggle, and all the suffering and disappointment as well as all the love and friendship and happiness, are quite accidental and meaningless, and just come to a sudden end the moment I die, and don't mean anything beyond that point at all ... well, I can only confess quite honestly that I myself would have to regard death as the most terrible enemy, a wicked and evil thing in itself. I should not then be able to believe in God at all – it would seem as if the whole of life was just a ghastly and meaningless accident.

John Williams's perspective, written all these years ago, is still shared by countless people. Like him, I knew at first hand all the beauty and strength available through faith. I was, after all, a Christian, wasn't I? I also had experience of bereavement early in life because I was forced to face the reality of death at the age of six, when my mother died.

The problem for me has never been so much the tragedies sometimes referred to as 'acts of God', but the capacity for evil emanating from the human condition itself – the crass obsessions, the greed, the inability to solve problems without violence ... the sheer lust for money and profit and power at the expense of ordinary folk, extending even into healthcare and the treatment of illness. Religious people call these phenomena 'sin' and 'evil'. When my physically and mentally healthy child died at her own hand, everything changed. I felt sucked back into a vortex of incomprehensible evil.

Suicidal thoughts

After the death of a child such thoughts are normal, and much more common than we assume. We hesitate to bring this topic up for discussion, and often for good reason. I recall the story of a terrible loss in the life of Katharine Hepburn, the unforgettable Hollywood star of my own childhood. When she was 12 years old a tragedy occurred, one that changed her life. During a trip to New York, Katharine and her brother Tom went to see a production of *A Connecticut Yankee in King Arthur's Court*, in which there is a hanging scene.

The next morning when Katharine went into her brother's room to wake him up, she found Tom hanged by his bedsheet from the rafters, already five hours' dead. Most probably it was a stunt gone wrong. He was 15. It is stark stories like these, added to the hunch that, rightly or wrongly, suicide may be somehow 'catching', that leads us to hesitate before too much talk about it – a paradox still unresolved in suicide prevention programmes.

When the topic of suicide arises in bereavement group discussions, and there is a request for a show of hands to ask how many in the group have had thoughts of suicide, a near-unanimous response is not unusual. One father told me of an overwhelming desire to rejoin his daughter, who lost her life while white-water rafting abroad, and whose body was never recovered. Every projectile, pill and potion seemed to him to exist for one purpose. These thoughts are very frightening in and of themselves, not least because suicide is self-execution. If there is one thing that people bereaved by their child's death for any reason know better than most, it is that the waves of damage following the death of a child are immense. An inner wisdom, a sense of responsibility to others outweighing personal pain, a loving community and, hopefully, an instinct for survival, however tenuous, are vital at these times.

There was one secret personal wish I let slip once and only once. As I mentioned earlier, I said to a friend that I wished Caitlin had survived even if she were brain-damaged, because I knew I'd still love her no matter how severely she was damaged, and I'd rather she still be alive just so I could still care for her. 'What do I do now with all this love?' I cried. My friend told me not to be so selfish and to get a grip. She didn't add, but I could hear the unsaid bit, that Caitlin was better off dead than brain-damaged. In the time that has passed since her death I have spoken to countless people who have loved their severely brain-damaged children, disabled to various degrees, and the dilemma remains. Had Caitlin survived with a severe disability, would it be a better sort of complete life change to all those around her, and especially to me, than has been caused by her death? But she did not survive. I do know now that there is a way of spreading the love around, and am resigned to the fact that the secret wish was indeed only theoretical anyway.

Memento mori

In a suspicious death there will be photographs taken by the police scenes-of-crime officer. I hadn't been able to bear to look at them when the coroner offered them for perusal at the inquest, but a few weeks later I wrote to him requesting copies of the photos. He refused. In another age we would probably have made a death mask, but all I knew was that these photos were the last ones taken of Caitlin, and I didn't feel that the police should possess the only copies. Caitlin had not been disfigured when we found her, and I'm sure I would have felt differently had this been the case.

I persisted in my request, and eventually the coroner agreed to allow me photocopies of the photographs in his possession. The copies were extremely poor. Four years later I still wanted proper copies and went through great hoops of bureaucracy to make yet another request. By this time Caitlin's records were held some distance away. Twice I was refused, until finally two photos were released, although not the photos I would have chosen. Lord knows what the police lawyer thought – that I planned some macabre media campaign perhaps? The issue of photographs became fraught in our case, because the last photos of Caitlin were taken by the police. The coroner, and later the police, have discretion to release photographs, and in our case my request passed through several hands of people who frankly didn't seem to know what to do with it, and made me feel abnormal for asking in the first place.

Apparitions

The philosopher Wittgenstein described faces as 'the soul of the body'. Think about the way you can pick out the face of your child or your friend from a sea of faces in any crowd anywhere in the world. No two alike. Some friends who have lost their child say they keep seeing them from the corner of the eye, crossing streets, moving ahead in the crowd. One friend said that after her son's death she kept seeing young men she thought were him, and to a distressing degree. Sylvia Pavey, now a bulwark in The Compassionate Friends UK, saw her son as clear as day, and again some time after his death, as she drove slowly in heavy traffic. Sylvia was glad of the vision.

Arranging the funeral

This comes by necessity at a time when bereaved families are the last people to be able to deal with it. We may well have never had anything to do with a funeral before. Some of us wish that we had known of choices available, because it is possible that we would have done things differently. After Caitlin's death we were fortunate in that because of the Easter season we had ten days to work things out carefully. The funeral director is also someone we know personally. We chose burial rather than cremation, which meant that we had to choose a place of burial. Our parish priest was extremely kind and helpful, and made suggestions for memorial carvers.

I wanted Caitlin to be wearing her favourite clothes – designer jeans and top, best trainers – and I wanted to dress her, and do her make-up in the way she would have liked. In the end it was her dear friend Jolene who helped us with Caitlin's hair and make-up. We could have requested a photograph, but did not know this at the time. Incidentally, it is important to let family and friends who wish to view the child's body know if there has been any significant change in appearance.

I requested time to spend alone with Caitlin's body in the chapel of rest; her father and brother visited her there too. On the day before the funeral, we brought her body home in order that friends could come and say goodbye. This was unusual in our community and there were whispers of 'not a proper thing to do', but we ignored this criticism and soldiered on. These are not times to give in to reproach of any kind. It was important to have her body in our care before the funeral. The funeral was held in our local parish church of St George's.

We had special music and arranged a sound system to carry it. Partly because Caitlin had family from all round the world, many of whom could not be present, my nephew Scott made a video of the funeral; for this we asked permission of our parish priest, and Scott was very discreet. I remain impressed that in spite of his own considerable distress, Scott filmed the funeral for absent loved ones.

We encouraged Caitlin's friends to wear bright colours and, it being April, bring spring flowers. Some time later I attended a friend's funeral where flowers were handed to mourners on arrival. I've also heard of the family asking for people to bring posies or single flowers from their own gardens. It is also common practice to have flowers from the family only, and ask for donations to a chosen charity instead.

Something I regret not doing for Caitlin's funeral was to have a book at the funeral in which people who attended could enter their names. The funeral director would have done this, I'm sure, but I did not request a book or cards to be distributed.

There are other choices. The British Humanist Association performs services as well as many religious organizations. Funerals can be held in the home, or in a crematorium chapel, where services are limited to 20–30-minute sessions. Bereaved mourners have sometimes felt that crematoria have rather a treadmill atmosphere about them, but this is not always the case. We were able to plan every aspect of Caitlin's funeral because there was time to do so. Bereaved families who cannot do the same can rely on clergy and funeral directors whose experience and guidance can be relied upon, asking for music and readings with a personal resonance to family and friends.

Funerals are expensive, and I was certainly in no state to be talking money with an undertaker. The savings account I had set up for Caitlin's university life covered some of it, and someone asked on my behalf about financial help with these costs. There are in the UK allowances and benefits available for those who need them, and the Benefits Agency publishes booklets: *What to do after a death in England and Wales/Scotland*. The purchase of burial plots is most often arranged by local councils or by parish clergy. Types of memorial stones and inscriptions are governed by regulations which vary from diocese to diocese.

The media

Somehow the moments pass and join up. We wake each morning and we still breathe. In our community the media tune in to emergency service airwaves and will know of, and possibly respond to, call-outs. The death of a young person is news, and suicide tends to be big news – 'If it bleeds, it leads.' This unpleasantly accurate maxim holds true in provincial outposts as well as in big towns. At 7 a.m. on the morning following Caitlin's suicide, a young woman reporter is at our front door. A friend turns her away, but later we hear that she has gone round the village asking about Caitlin's death – trying to speak to the vicar, the publican, the newsagent. Just doing her job.

I was neither willing nor capable of giving an interview to the media about Caitlin, but that didn't stop them making something up as best they could. When inaccuracies occurred we decided to ignore them, our reasoning being that sending in corrections might lead to follow-up stories. It helped to a degree that journalism is for me a familiar craft; after all, journalists have a job to do, to fill a space on a page with something readable, credible and sometimes even helpful.

In retrospect, I would recommend that the family release a brief statement, possibly with a photograph of the child, as one way of trying to ensure that accurate information, and not too much information, will be published. But the pressures we are under at this time are largely dictated by forces outside our control, and at the time it did not occur to me to release a statement. We did, though, put obituary notices in relevant local and national newspapers:

Suddenly, at home.
Caitlin Elizabeth Rosalie Hurcombe, Monday 6th April 1998,
beloved daughter of Linda and Tom and sister of Sean.
'I'd rather spend one day as a tiger than the rest of my
life as a potato.'

The quote at the end was from Caitlin's diary. When she told me how much she liked it as a motto, ever the typical English teacher I pointed out that she was mixing metaphors, animal with vegetable. Caitlin's reply was, 'Yep. Exactly what I mean.' In a moment of amusing ineptitude the local newspaper rang to say they were concerned about the quote – 'Was your daughter mentally handicapped?' 'No. Why do you ask?' After ringing off I thought, anyway, so what if she *had* been 'handicapped'!

Caitlin was a big-time babysitter and adored looking after

children. They flocked round her like ducklings wherever she went, and her little friends in our village were many. Notes began slipping through the door, and were usually illustrated: 'Dear Caitlin, What's it like in heaven with God and all the famous angels? Love Sadie.' 'Dear Caitlin, Why did you die? You were going to drive me in a car when you got your licence. Charles xx.' 'Dear Caitlin, You always make me smile and now I have to cry. Love Annie.'

And many more that I cannot recall. We placed a special wicker basket, festooned with bright ribbons, outside the front door for Caitlin's friends to place letters, notes and trinkets. Because we live on a busy village high street, we did this in part to keep down the number of people coming through the door; but also I felt unable to bear seeing all the children and helping them at that time with their questions. I had planned to copy these notes into a little book for Caitlin's young friends. Somehow I forgot to do this; and when we buried her, I lowered the wicker basket filled with its poems and drawings into the grave to rest on her coffin. It was a way of placing letters of the children's love as close to Caitlin as possible. A friend teased me gently, reminding me of a story about the poet Dante Gabriel Rossetti. When Rossetti's wife of two years, Elizabeth Siddal, died of an overdose of laudanum, Rossetti buried the only complete manuscript of his poems with her body. Some seven years later he exhumed and published them. 'Well,' I replied, 'these poems weren't mine, they were the children's and written to Caitlin, so I won't be digging them up.'

Before Caitlin's funeral we had time make announcements in both the local and national press, and to prepare the kind of funeral that would properly mourn Caitlin and take into account her many friends and loved ones. If I have one wish I could grant to suffering parents, family and friends during such loss, it is that you be surrounded by loved ones, as we were. You will still feel alone, but you will be better off being alone with one another. Friends will cook, wash up, fetch and carry, pray, sing, even tell gentle sweet jokes. This is a miracle of the commonplace which for me embodies all that is best in being human.

Our friends took up a collection, a substantial amount; someone had remembered that we were self-employed and without any earnings during this time. This was invaluable – you forget about money at a time like this – and incalculably thoughtful. For one thing it enabled us to provide food for people who travelled hundreds, and even thousands, of miles to come to the funeral. I want to tread lightly on the advice line, but here is some anyway. I would say, don't let false pride convince you that you should never be 'beholden' to anyone or accept money from friends. If it is relevant to you, give your friends 'the gift' of receiving their offerings graciously, money included.

Emily Dickinson said that 'after great pain, a formal feeling comes', and for me this was entirely accurate in the days while we prepared for the funeral. Favourite surrogate brother Richard brought a bottle of single malt whiskey, and over an eight-hour period I sipped half the bottle away, hoping, I think, either to feel something or perhaps nothing. Nothing was what happened. In normal circumstances I would be on the floor with such a quantity in my system – more accurately, I wouldn't have been drinking such an amount of alcohol in any remotely normal circumstances. But now when I wished for the oblivion of drunkenness, my body said no. There is no way out, only through. No drug, no balm, exists to deal with this one. Get a grip, Linda. Bear up. You are in a script from hell that neither you or anybody can or would want to play. Do it.

Feelings of isolation may appear insuperable. I was in turn consumed by frenetic energy and then tired beyond imagining. I felt drawn back into a vortex of diminishment – helpless, useless, inconsolable. For the sake of friends I think I pretended, so that loved ones weren't drawn into my maw of despair, the cold rage and feelings of abandonment. They may have an entirely different take on this. I daren't ask.

Although I was 'all hugged out', I let myself be hugged and held and pampered. Inside, it was this – I was shrunken, raw and short of breath, and it felt as if the weight on my chest had broken my heart. The very thought of living with such pain through the next five minutes, much less for the rest of my life, made me suicidal. I had no control whatsoever over these feelings.

Charlie Walton, in *When There Are No Words* (Walton, 1996), describes this sheer physical weight and its effect on his breathing:

> There was another physical phenomenon that I could never have anticipated. It's that pair of invisible cement blocks that someone ties together and loops over your shoulders . . . the ropes come to rest on your two shoulders and the length of the ropes is perfectly measured to assure that the two blocks will press in . . . from front

to back . . . on your lungs. It is *possible* to breathe with the blocks on your shoulders . . . but not to breathe deeply.

Charlie says that it is virtually impossible to explain this burden on breathing to anyone who hasn't experienced the breathlessness of deep grief. In Charlie's experience this physical difficulty in breathing began to ease about three weeks after the boys died. Shock knocks some of us into a merciful oblivion and we don't remember anything during this time. Medication, given in the mistaken belief that grief and depression are the same condition, can increase amnesia. I'm preaching here what I didn't practise, but if I had to do it all again I'd turn down the kind offers of temazepam and beta blockers.

In retrospect, and even as I write this, I detach from what I am feeling to be able to say it, but it is necessary to do so. It is clear that grief, like all processes of growth, is a dynamic rather than decaying phenomenon, a moving through and growing round. Sometimes we go forward, sometimes back – and sometimes we get 'stuck' for a time. But a process is a process, and change is one of the unchangeable truths of life. We will continue to grow, to grow older and perhaps wiser. We will, like our child, also be dead someday. The loss of meaning that comes with the death of our child is greater than any we could imagine, but we will have to invent new meanings. The choice is stark; choose life after your child's death, or curl up and die because of the loss. The latter is tempting, but the former is the correct choice. I kept saying to myself, 'Therefore choose life. Therefore choose life. Therefore choose life.'

We are told that this growth comes in stages, which include the following emotions: shock, denial, anger, bargaining with God, depression and, finally, acceptance. The great pioneer of grief and bereavement, Elisabeth Kübler-Ross, first identified these stages, but I believe she would be dismayed to see their elevation to iconic status. We know that we may not experience all the stages, and in any case not in a given order, although shock and disbelief do often come first. We cannot *believe* that this has happened to us, to our child. These things happen to other people who we read about in the newspapers. The shock affects mind, body, spirit, our whole being. The physical marks lower the blood pressure, make the skin cold, the heart quickens; we feel an acute sense of horror. We may suffer a variety of physical complaints: headaches, nausea, heightened alarm or panic – or we may feel dead inside. These states paradoxically may hold the pain at bay and allow us to carry on with what must be done, to carry on with arrangements for the funeral and what follows.

Feeling anger

This is an extremely important emotion, and because Caitlin died by suicide I was urged by others to allow my anger towards her to surface. But I never felt angry with Caitlin. I felt angry about teen bullies and drug companies and youth magazines touting erotically illiterate information – and with the friends who advised me repeatedly to be angry with her! I explained as best I could that I had been plenty angry at Caitlin when she was alive, when the anger had a purpose. This said, it remains true that anger is often frowned upon when it should not be.

So, if you are angry after the death of your child, it's because you have been hurt beyond your wildest imagination. An outrage has occurred. Sometimes we can't find a focus for our anger, and lash out at innocent people ... doctors, funeral directors, friends. Sometimes the fury can be random. It's probably a good idea to recognize anger and use it positively if possible. I'm not saying that this is easy, but there are ample injustices in this painful world, not to mention the problems on our very doorstep, to work on.

When our child dies, suddenly or otherwise, everything we believed in seems destroyed. 'Will I recognize the person I will now become?' 'Will the people who love me want to know this person I am becoming now?' We truly believed that we could protect our child from anything. We were loving caring parents and now our child is dead. *We have failed to save our child's life.* But, but. We did the best we could, our very best. We would have given our own lives to save our child's life. But life isn't always fair. You may feel you are going mad – personally, I wanted madness but felt an 'incurable sanity' gripping me and forcing me to face each moment, like a rabbit frozen in the headlights of a car that frames and contains me in time. Even in the darkest most hellish times, I also wanted to take responsibility as a witness to Caitlin's intrinsic worth as a human being despite her death by suicide.

Indeed, we will never be the same. This is a painful fact, not least because we may well not like the person we seem to be becoming. Don't be afraid to shed tears for the loss not only of your precious child, but to mourn the loss of the person you were when your child was alive. The qualities eluding me after several years are spontaneity and delight. I know these existed and continue to exist all around me, but I can't *feel* them. Things are more formal – and fearless – these days. I find myself afraid of nothing, which can be positive, but not when I'm driving on the motorway and want to go faster, and faster, and faster. At this point the formality 'angel' kicks in – 'Linda, slow down. This is dangerous behaviour in a woman of your age.'

Distractedness

Another extremely disorienting part of raw or 'unprocessed' grief is the inability to concentrate. What was it that I just read? What did my friend just tell me? Why am I in this room? Where are we supposed to be going? A personal blessing of this time for me was a sense of humour. My best friend pointed out that at least I was as goofy as ever and, however stricken with fear, we did laugh. We laughed at the hospital 'chapel' when we saw the way the mortician had dressed Caitlin, in a frilly white choirgirl's gown which looked like a parody of a high-church vicar's chasuble, when in fact Caitlin was a 'fashionista' teen who loved labels and messages on the outside of her clothes, fond of Gap and Quiksilver and FCUK. I could hear her voice clear as a bell: 'Get me outta this tacky gear NOW, Mum!'

We passed around the 'bush telegraph' that we were bringing Caitlin's body home on the night before the funeral to let her friends know they were welcome to come to her home and say their goodbyes. This seemed right and proper, not least because of the sudden nature of her death. In our small community the undertakers were our friends; they built Caitlin's coffin and prepared her body for burial. When the coffin arrived, several friends were there with us helping us to decide, among other things, where to place it. My son's godmother Sue came up with an idea: 'Let's put the coffin in front of the telly. Caitlin was always lying there on the couch watching it whenever I came over.' We laughed through our tears, and turned on the television for a bit.

This night of vigil was long and intense. People came and went, chatted and left. Several brought small items to place in the coffin: a lock of hair, a ring, a flacon of Samsara, Caitlin's favourite perfume. Her friend Jolene, who helped us dress and apply Caitlin's make-up, asked if she could swap her own gold charm bracelet with Caitlin's, and of course I said yes. The gifts included drawings, a restaurant menu, even a tin of lager. We were in effect treating Caitlin as if she were still alive – instinctively, I believe, taking a last opportunity to 'do something' symbolically for her body before the time of burial when such creative pretence would be less sustainable.

'Talking the talk, walking the walk'

My dear friends. Letting me talk and talk and talk, tell Caitlin's story over and over and over. And *doing* things. We let them *do* things, serve us, an extended family of doers, feeders, cleaners, planners. I'm a bit of a loner at times, so it was not always easy to welcome this help when all I wanted to do was curl up and die myself. But I needed these friends, not least because I was intensely suicidal. What stopped me killing myself were friends gently pointing out that they loved me and needed me – and did I want to have them feeling the way about losing me that I felt about losing Caitlin? The answer was an emphatic no, that although I thought I wanted oblivion, I did not want anyone to have to feel what I was feeling.

Sleep and dreams

What about sleeping and dreaming? We will all dream, and some of us will remember our dreams. I dreamed of Caitlin most nights, still do. In dreams she is all ages, including living to be a grown-up and having babies. In the early days after her death the dreams were most often of her resuscitation. Example: Caitlin's own GP arrives at the scene of her suicide. 'Has she been breathing?' asks the doctor. 'No, not for a while now,' I reply. Dr Gray quickly opens her case, pulls out some electrodes and attaches them to Caitlin's head. 'These should do the trick,' she says, smiling. Next thing, Caitlin is sitting up saying she'd love some pasta please. The obvious problem with such dreams is waking up.

Writing

I kept an erratic journal of dreams because my spiritual director suggested I try to write for at least ten minutes a day after I told her that I was literally lost for words. No words? A wordophile writer without words? Yes, I said. I am shtoom. There was life before Caitlin died – life after Caitlin died. Her death seemed to be the final word on anything that had ever happened, the *only* thing that had ever happened. There were no words for the 'after'. Yet, trying to follow Una's advice, I wrote on 31 September 1998:

> My occasional journal has always been a total treat. Writing and sketching was as delightful as a meal with good friends. Now it bears a terror and I feel exhausted even thinking about it. 'In the beginning was the Word. What will I do without words?'

Words on pages have gradually returned, in non-fiction, but not in fiction. Two novels in the process of being revised for agent and publishers have lain dormant, five years on. 'Too many words in the world,' says my tongue-tied muse. I cannot say to my daughter, who was my inspiration but now long in the grave, Caitlin my muse, come forth! Many grieving families experience the opposite. Words of great depth and love come pouring out on the page. It has been a privilege to read and publish hundreds of such documents while editing the quarterly journal of The Compassionate Friends.

The gravestone

A week after the funeral our friend Judy called, pressed £100 into my palm, and packed me off, accompanied by Caitlin's dog Gus, to my good friend Michael's place on Ireland's west coast. I'd been going on about trying to find a wild stone for Caitlin's grave and wanted to check out Connemara marble and other colours. Michael took me all over the place, including a Connemara quarry. In the end I decided against the slightly, to my eye, lurid green of the Connemara marble I saw. I'll never forget the monument outside the quarry: 'This monument, erected 21 October 1896. On this day nothing happened.' I returned home a few days later 'unstoned', but the idea of an unfinished wild stone had seduced me. There was no rush. The gravediggers in our churchyard said it was a good idea to let the grave rest and any subsidence to settle for a year. In the end I turned down the artisans officially recommended by our parish priest, and opted for Will and Lottie O'Leary, a local couple who are both stone carvers (see Helpful Contacts at the back of the book). We have since become firm friends.

Will O'Leary seemed to know, without the exchange of too many words, what I was looking for. He took me to a Welsh valley called Corys, to a slate quarry, and we literally walked miles on a grey day, until, having stopped to rest, I discovered myself standing on a large hunk of black slate, long ago blasted from the mountainside and left unused to meld with the landscape. 'This is the one,' I said. Will wrote 'O'Leary' in chalk on the slate and ordered it to be delivered to his studio. He and Lottie carved Caitlin's stone; and the riven side, scored by the ancient movements of earth in graceful waves, bears the inscription 'BLESS HER SPIRIT'. On the finished reverse side of the stone, Lottie carved a profile of Caitlin's dog Gus, gazing up at the constellation Sirius, whose main star is the Dog Star or hound of heaven, the brightest star in our hemisphere. A simple rectangular plaque in heather slate settles at the foot of the wild stone:

Caitlin Elizabeth
Rosalie Hurcombe.
Died 6th April 1998 aged 19 years.

I go most days to Caitlin's grave. It is a normal part of daily prayers and walks with the dogs. I'm sure that many of us, believers and non-believers alike, find solace in cemeteries. A great deal of love is carved there for all to see. The brevity of our time on earth. The perspective on the journey and mystery beyond the grave. You see the transience of even words dug into stone, and the constancy of change.

Facing the inquest

Inquests can be particularly nightmarish to the uninitiated, not least because of the Alice-in-Wonderland-ish rules of the court, combined with the sweeping powers of the coroner (TCF, 1997); an important coroner's review is taking place as this book goes to press.

23 June 1998

The inquest into Caitlin's death was held on this date in Bishops Castle Market Hall in Shropshire. When Caitlin was alive I only ever knew it as the place where the weekly produce market happened. We arrived like automatons, seeing none of the stalls piled high with fresh vegetables, fruit and bric-à-brac that were usually placed round the perimeter. However, I couldn't help noticing an abandoned carrot in a corner of the room. I owe to that carrot the disappearance of fear – somehow a small vegetable put things in perspective for me.

Before the inquest I had requested that the coroner let me know what he would be discussing; he declined to do so. If the case were criminal and I were implicated, I would have understood his response. In the event, I wanted to be prepared for what I was going to hear, but this was not to be. I think in retrospect that this is a cruel and unnecessary twiddling of legality for no purpose.

The policeman who attended on the night of Caitlin's death, and witnessed her postmortem, had asked me to arrive half-an-hour early for the inquest; he told me that he had given the newspapers the wrong time, so that hopefully we wouldn't have to put up with the added stress of media presence. I later learned that he stuck out his neck to do this on our behalf, as inquests are legally in the public arena. Anyone can attend. Friends, my brother, my partner Trish, strangers gather in the room that is clumsily revamped into the semblance of a ramshackle courtroom: up front a platform with a desk and chair for the coroner, the rest of us in rows on stiff, creaky wooden chairs.

The coroner arrived a few minutes late; we stood as he took his place. He delivered a lengthy homily on the purpose of an inquest: not to blame, not to establish liability, either civil or criminal, simply to answer four questions:

- Who died?
- How did they die?
- When did they die?
- Where did they die?

The 'whys' and undercurrents are not part of the equation. So you go through this: Where did she live? How did she die? What time did the doctor say she was dead? Who identified her when the police arrived? Where did the death occur? There was a statement from the scenes-of-crime photographer. The coroner asked if I wished to view the photographs. I declined, although I did very much wish to see these photographs, the last of my daughter on this earth. I just didn't want to look at them in full view of the other people gathered at the inquest. The pathologist reported on the postmortem. Described method of death as 'mild compression of upper larynx', and said 'the person didn't suffer'. Only substance in body was consistent with a 'therapeutic dose of fluoxetine hydrochloride (Prozac)'. That was it. We dutifully answered the questions the coroner had extrapolated from statements made earlier to the police.

About three weeks after the inquest I began to see that Caitlin's antidepressant medication might be implicated in her radical change in character and her violent self-inflicted death, and wrote a note in my journal to this effect.

Consulting psychics and mediums

There are people called psychics or mediums who claim they can contact the dead. They maintain that they possess special powers that enable (even obligate) them to do what few people are able to do – reach the 'other side' and communicate with those who have died (Baugher, 1998). Is this possible? Are all who claim these powers capable of doing what seems to be beyond normal human ability? Are some of these people knowingly deceiving a highly vulnerable group, the bereaved? Are there a few true mediums who have bridged the gap between life and death, heaven and earth? Bereaved people are notoriously vulnerable, as witnessed by the huge financial exploitation surrounding funeral arrangements. There are the good, the bad and the ugly. The same probably holds true for mediums.

Some friends were bemused when I told them I was planning to visit a Christian medium after Caitlin's death. One friend quipped that in her opinion the terms 'Christian' and 'medium' were a contradiction in terms – to which another replied, 'better a Christian medium than a medium Christian'. I treasured that remark not only for its non-judgemental kindness, but because, fortunately, the medium confirmed important and very private things for me.

We all have personal beliefs about what happens after death.

Some people believe that with the right means we can contact our dead children and, moreover, that it is quite proper to do so. Part of the pain of the death of someone we love is the realization that we will never again be able to hear and hold and argue and, quite simply, *nurture* them.

What did I want from a medium? I wanted knowledge from an objective observer who knew nothing about me or my circumstances, and who could translate messages from dead people. In brief, although I knew Caitlin was somewhere, I wanted reassurance that she was OK. Looking back, I confess that the demons of taboo were deep inside my head regarding suicide, the lurking notion that suicide is the ultimate sin against the spirit of life, rendering the 'committer' of this act a lost soul.

Justine Picardie's superlative book, *If the Spirit Moves You* (Picardie, 2002), depicts a sister's grief over the death from cancer of her younger sister, Ruth. She traces the upheaval in family life after Ruth's death, but mainly the book is the story of one person's navigation through grief. An important part of the story is the floundering experienced in the early stages of bereavement. Justine misses Ruth's voice as much as everything else, and experiments with an impressive variety of spiritual phenomena – and some pretty dodgy operators too. She attends seances, consults mediums, even writes e-mails to Ruth – Ruth@heaven.com. All this uncannily accurate depiction of the feelings of being lost in the first months and years of bereavement is remarkably free of judgement. You, the reader, wouldn't decide against visiting a medium because you had read Justine's book. One contact, a rather legendary British medium called Rita Rogers, seems to make some uncanny and useful remarks via a telephone 'reading'. On the whole, though, one doesn't know whether these various people helped Justine to discover what brought a semblance of peace in the end – what you do know is that Ruth and her memory have become part of Justine and will never be wholly lost.

To those who wish to consult a medium while maintaining a healthy scepticism, the following suggestions may be useful (Baugher, 1998):

- Tape-record everything, including the phone call when you make the appointment.
- Speak first to other bereaved parents who may have considered

this option. Take a friend with you if you feel comfortable doing so.

- Prepare five 'no doubt' questions, and begin the session with these questions. For example: 'Can you tell me who it is I wish to contact?'
- Watch for a medium's 'false tricks'. Included among these are:
  - Putting statements in question form that could apply to almost anyone, e.g. 'Was there a drug or alcohol problem?' This could apply to most families.
  - Widening the terms of reference. If you said 'no' to a previous question, you may hear, 'I'm getting some sort of abuse, maybe physical or emotional or abusive words'.
  - Another tactic is 'letter' or 'name' fishing, e.g. 'I'm getting the letter R. Who is this?' Or 'Who is George? Or Fred?' Most of us know someone with these names.
  - The bereaved often wear jewellery and clothing of the loved one who has died. Mediums often ask 'Who is wearing his shirt?' or 'Where are the earrings?'
  - Asking if you've lost something. If you say 'no', the medium may suggest you've forgotten.

If you wish to contact a medium there are two paths – one is to believe and to accept what you are told at face value. The other is to attend with tough questions and not be too disappointed if what you see at face value is not what you wished to hear. Your child or sibling may well want you to be sceptical – I know Caitlin would.

Meditation on suffering

C. S. Lewis said in *A Grief Observed* (Lewis, 1961): 'He [God] always knew that my temple [i.e. Lewis's good fortune and love of 'H'] was a house of cards. His only way of making *me* realize the fact was to knock it down.'

I can relate to that, as I've always balked at the idea of unmerited suffering. I remember asking my grandmother why Jesus had to get nailed to the cross when he was so nice to everyone – why couldn't he be like her, my Mama Morris, and get old so that even more people could find out how cool he was? At this point I wasn't asking why God killed God's self in sending Jesus to die, but more, why was it necessary for human beings to kill God in order to be redeemed? Hadn't human history shown us to be the world's most dangerous and nasty mammal? Choose life! Enough killing. Flawed theology perhaps, but crucial to my entire life's work as mother, teacher, student and worker in the peace movement.

The word 'patient' derives from the Latin 'to suffer' – bearing pains or trials calmly or without complaint; able or willing to bear up. Bereaved parents are no strangers to suffering. We bear the sharpest end of it, patiently or otherwise, in the loss of our child.

The received wisdom amid all the natural bounty of our world is that innocent suffering is redemptive – and we hear well-meaning reassurances that the death of our child need not have been 'in vain', that memories and a belief in renewal will be helpful. Yet in my personal spiritual perspective, which is Christian, I experience difficulty in being comforted by the thought of redemptive suffering and death. The reason for this is primal; it does not bring my child back. Nothing can do that. There is a promise of reunion, but it doesn't bring my child back to life on earth, and so even as a believer I reluctantly admit that the story is of little private comfort . . . 'O me of little faith!'

Apparently I am not strong enough to be ennobled by great suffering. I continue to choke on the term 'in vain', because it *feels* that the loss of my child *was* senseless, was indeed in vain. 'A wounded deer . . . leaps highest' said the poet Emily Dickinson. Unless, I retort, she's been shot in the legs. I continue to work on this 'bad attitude', and the consolation from loved ones is considerable and oh so necessary. The glimpses of glory I thank them for, daily.

Stupid words

In the early days after the loss of a child, lovely concerned people, who are not stupid, can say some pretty stupid things to grieving parents and families. Here are some things *not* to say to grieving parents, *especially* in the first days or weeks. All of the following have either been said to me, or to friends who have lost a child.

DON'T:
- Quote verses of Scripture like, 'His yoke is easy and his burden is light.'

- Make a comparison with the horse, dog, hamster, axolotl, cat or budgerigar whose death is wrenching your soul at the moment.
- Comment on how nice it was that enough people came to the funeral to do it justice.
- Quote the Scott Holland poem that begins with the line 'Death is nothing at all . . . ' The poem has its place and it is usually not here, with the death of a child.
- Tell us not to feel guilty.
- Tell us it's not our fault.
- Tell us we are fortunate to have another child or children.
- Tell us to get on and have another child, get a pet, buy a hat.
- Tell us our child is at peace, troubles over at last.
- Say how marvellous it is to see us coping so well with such an 'awful business'.
- Say that the best thing is to keep busy.
- Say that we'll soon be back to our old selves and 'get over it'.
- Say that you know exactly how we feel. This may be true, but it doesn't help.

You're probably thinking, 'But some of these things are true! What *can* I say that will be appropriate?' and you're right. The list may seem terribly rigid, and I've long forgiven and forgotten who said what . . . mostly. The fact is, though, that there are indeed no words, no words, no words. If a word could be a hug, or a song, or a group of like-minded sufferers who understand how we truly feel, and will be there for the long run through thick and thin, well yes. The best words are probably, starkly, 'I'm so sorry. I cannot imagine your loss.' Frances Dominica, in *Just My Reflection* (Dominica, 1997), is most succinct: 'Those who have themselves experienced a similar type of bereavement can help as no one else can; the rest of us should guard against saying, "I know how you feel" – we don't.'

Grief and depression

Many of us while in the depths of grief have turned to medication for depression to help us. I did. But it is necessary to point out that grief is not the same thing as depression. For starters, grief doesn't just come and go every few months or years, but instead is a specific response to the death of the loved one.

Defining depression is a notoriously difficult business. Looking back over four centuries at what has been written about depression, we find that only quite recently has the condition been thought of as an illness – that is, become medicalized. Instead – as Dorothy Rowe explains in *Depression: The Way Out of Your Prison* (Rowe, 2001) – depression, or melancholia, was thought of as anger turned inwards, a lack of wisdom in living, and a lack of self-knowledge.

The suggested cures for depression over the centuries have been manifold:

- living in moderation;
- recognizing one's unique susceptibilities;
- eating a proper diet;
- sleeping and physical exercise;
- avoiding the known triggers that plunge one into the abyss;
- being part of a supportive family, social and community network;
- preparing to face adversity;
- taking personal responsibility and initiative to live with care.

There is no doubt that severe depression can sometimes be provoked by bereavement, but it is wrong – and quite possibly an insult – to assume that a bereaved parent or relative is suffering from depression. Though there are symptomatic similarities, the condition of grief is life-changing on every level – physical, moral and spiritual; and depression may or may not be one aspect of it. Fundamental notions of meaning and purpose, the human condition itself – all our beliefs are called into question when a child dies:

- What does it mean to be mortal?
- What does it mean that everyone I love is mortal?
- Does life have meaning?
- Why do we suffer?
- Why do bad things happen to good people?
- Is there any meaning in suffering?
- Is life anything more than a cruel joke?
- What role does fate play in our lives?
- Why am I still alive when she/he is dead?

In the midst of this profound spiritual crisis (not necessarily religious in any institutional sense) exists a struggle on every level of our being. For the grieving person, feelings of depression may be just one component of the larger problem of loss:

- Longing
- Survivor guilt
- General guilt
- Shame
- Anger
- Shock
- Denial
- Loneliness
- Fear
- Rage

Added to all the above feelings is the indisputable knowledge that the child for whose life we would happily give our own is gone and will never come back.

If babies die of incurable diseases and we can become ex-parents in a matter of seconds, how can we trust life at all, much less a loving divine God who is good and all-powerful? This is what has happened to our beloved person. How can we feel safe or secure in the knowledge that the earth will remain on its axis or gravity hold? Absolutely nothing seems safe or trustworthy, not even that the sun will rise in the east tomorrow.

Grief for a lost child is a crisis of the entire human condition into which we are born and to which we try to establish some sense of order and trust. Besides the sheer inexplicable emotional pain, in grief our intellectual understandings are cracked wide open, forcing us to our knees and to what may be left of our original spark. We may be overwhelmed with doubt, even the most faithful. We are deluged with this loss; we are lost and we are losers too.

An entire reworking of beliefs will need to take place, and from the ground up. Those from a Judeo-Christian background may have been raised on the belief that if we work hard, pay our taxes and try to live a good moral life, we will prosper and good things will come to us. We probably feel that inexplicable death or loss should not have come to good, law-abiding, God-fearing citizens and believers!

A philosophy of life that can incorporate the actuality of unfair, undeserved catastrophe is not easy to formulate. It takes hard and courageous searching of the soul. It requires exhausting questionings and exploring. It demands constant reworking, and often the help of professionals (counsellors, psychotherapists and/or clergy). In addition, grief often excludes those systems, beliefs and friends we used to count on for discourse, so it can be a lonely and relentless quest.

Yet, time and again, I have seen brave, tenacious people find a way to become 'better rather than bitter'. All the truisms work: that the only way out of grief is through it; that we don't get over it, we become accustomed to it, by carrying the loss and holding it within the continuing bonds forged by our revised beliefs and rebuilt lives.

Medications and alcohol

Experiencing bereavement at its most acute brings a natural desire for respite from profound pain. Although easier said than done – I for one certainly did not go medication- or alcohol-free – it is best to avoid any prolonged use of tranquillizers, antidepressants and alcohol. This is because the drugs only mask the grief and will most likely prolong the process. It is a fact that no simplistic treatment will 'cure' grief. However painful, grief is best handled when we are awake, not drugged to oblivion. You may be offered medication to help you cope with your bereavement. When you feel ready to stop, it is very important that you do so in consultation with your physician, since over-rapid withdrawal can cause problems for some people, and may be medically hazardous, particularly for older persons.

The strange and difficult paradox of early – and indeed ongoing – grief is harsh and continuing. Accept help from your friends in the early and ongoing days of grieving. Most importantly, face yourself in the mirror and say you did the best you could. Choose life.

3

Baby

A baby is God's opinion that life should go on.
(Carl Sandburg)

Our lives are defined by those we have lost.
(author unknown)

A wanted baby, born safely, is an unquestionable gift given by a man and a woman to one another and to the world. The days on which our son Sean and daughter Caitlin were born were the happiest of my life. No competition. Given this view, I should therefore have been better prepared for the sick feeling that gripped me as I read one of the daily broadsheets one fine spring morning. Headlined 'The Many Faces of Death', the article described heart-rending stories of some 100 people who had died, often by stray bullets, in the Iraq war; they were considered 'collateral damage' in this pre-emptive attack. Five of those mentioned in the article who died were babies, plus a number of children aged between 4 and 12.

War death statistics, stark as they are, are dwarfed by daily domestic deaths happening to families worldwide. In England and Wales alone, more children die of sudden infant death in a year (although cot deaths have mercifully reduced in recent years) than all who die of cancer, heart disease, pneumonia, child abuse, AIDS, cystic fibrosis and muscular dystrophy combined. There are so many stories crying out to be heard. It is not possible to tell them all – a throng of unique human beings, pressing to board this small vessel, already full up.

Stillborn babies

Statistics on neonatal deaths vary, but we can reliably say that approximately 1 in every 115 births is a stillbirth. They outnumber Sudden Infant Death Syndrome by 10 to 1. In 2001 the infant mortality rate fell to 5.5 deaths per 1,000 live births from 5.6 per 1,000 in 2000 in England and Wales. These figures reflect a long-term decline (Office of National Statistics), which is good news, and long may the trend continue.

Yet sometimes the obvious needs saying: each statistic, writes Elaine Storkey in *Losing a Child: Finding a Path through the Pain* (Storkey, 1999), represents a human life, a real person. Statistics mean nothing at all to a bereaved family. Even a discredited twentieth-century dictator like Joseph Stalin recognized that 'A single death is a tragedy, a million deaths is a statistic.' In bereavement, the grief and pain are mine, and in the case of the death of a child there are never two of anyone. William Blake knew this better than most:

> To see a world in a grain of sand
> And a Heaven in a Wild Flower
> Hold Infinity in the palm of your hand
> And Eternity in an hour ...

Even the youngest child will have had a unique personality, presence and individuality – a stamp of being herself/himself and absolutely none other.

Parents who bring stillborn children into the world generally receive no public recognition of their baby's death. Too often the loss is seen, even by medical staff, as a foetus that didn't make it through, rather than a living being who has died. After a baby born still, Bel Mooney reflected in a piece called 'The Light of Experience':

> There is no divine right to happiness, simply a duty to cope, to understand and to love ... I do not wish to 'get over' his loss, nor do I wish to replace him with more children. I simply wish that his life and death should be absorbed into my own; enlarging and deepening in perception. (TCF newsletter, March 1977)

The feelings of parents bereaved by babies who are born still, or who die not long after birth, are similar to other sudden and unexpected deaths – those of shock and utter loss. Too often these feelings are compounded by the reactions of friends and family who don't know how to comfort the grieving couple. One friend put it this way: 'People don't like to think that babies die, but they do. I found during the first few weeks after Poppy's death that even my close friends and family were unhappy to talk about her. I think they thought my pain would go away if she was just "out of the picture".' This is not what usually happens, though. 'They kept urging us to get on with making another baby.' Sometimes friends and well-wishers can be extraordinarily insensitive – in thinking and perhaps even saying – that a new baby will somehow wipe out the earlier loss, that everything will be 'all right' when a 'replacement' has arrived. It is hard to have to explain that a new baby can never replace the child who has died, can never repair the rent that was torn in the fabric of life. A new child is of course welcome as a blessing and joy – but for himself or herself, not as a substitute.

The New Natural Death Handbook (Albery *et al.*, 1997) contained an excellent article capturing my admiration. Originally published in the *Guardian*, it is titled 'In Living Memory', and is written by Caroline Jay. Although it is heartening to observe that many of Caroline's experiences will be less common now than even a few years ago, many families – and especially mothers bereaved of newborn babies – will recognize and confirm her observations. For this reason, I have quoted from the article at length:

I was happy, healthy, seven and a half months pregnant and full of expectations. Within the space of 12 hours, struggling to shake off the effects of a general anaesthetic and an emergency Caesarean section, I was left holding my seemingly perfect stillborn daughter, Laura.

The four days that followed were spent being studiously avoided in a corner of the antenatal ward, desperately trying to shut out the sight of pregnant women and the sound of newborn babies crying. Still quite poorly and in a state of shock, I leapt at the opportunity for the hospital to make all Laura's funeral arrangements for me – anything to have the whole nightmare taken away.

The result was a totally meaningless cremation service taken by a stranger exactly one week to the minute after her birth; there was no gravestone, no special place of hers that I could visit and care for. Most importantly, there was the guilt and regret. I felt I had failed my daughter in the one and only thing I was ever going to be able to do for her.

Four years on, I know that my experience and feelings are not uncommon. I run a local branch of SANDS, the Stillbirth and

Neo-Natal Death Society (see Helpful Contacts at the back of the book). The aim is to support people whose babies die at or around birth by offering a listening ear and a shared experience. I want to make some good come out of the tragedy of Laura's death by trying to ensure that others don't end up with the same regrets as I did.

For example, I had absolutely no idea that I could have asked to hold Laura again a few hours or even a day or more later – at a time when I could have taken her in better and stored my memories of her. As it was, the only time I spent with her I was so dopey that I could barely lift my hand to stroke her face. I had no idea that I could have asked for a lock of her plentiful hair. Things are much better now ... but there is still room for improvement.

A national SANDS survey showed that while some hospitals handle the situation well, others do not. The practice of incinerating 'foetal material' along with hospital waste has not been completely stopped. Parents are not consulted and are ... totally unaware of the fate of their baby's body. Obviously it would be inappropriate, and in some cases quite wrong, to suggest that all babies lost through miscarriage should be held by their mothers. However, babies can be perfectly formed little beings long before they reach 28 weeks; I would suggest that they are most definitely not 'hospital waste fit for incineration only' and it is not the right of hospital staff to decide whether or not a mother should hold her child or decide upon the fate of its body; she should at least be told that she has a choice.

Just as holding your dead child plays an important part in the grieving process, so does saying a formal goodbye in the shape of a funeral or some other social ritual, be it religious or not. It is a way of sharing, of acknowledging the existence of, the child you have lost. This is especially true in the case of babies because society is keen to pretend they never existed ('Oh well, dear, you can just have another one' ... 'At least you've got your other children' ... 'As soon as the next one's born healthy everything will be all right'). The more people around me negated Laura's existence, the more they implied that other things would make up for her loss, the more I fought to keep her memory alive.

For women who have had miscarriages or terminations for abnormality, society offers even less opportunity to say goodbye

– after all, the baby didn't really ever exist, did it? But a loss is a loss and needs to be grieved for, needs to be acknowledged. Women who lost babies several years ago or more have to live with the fact that the infants' bodies were simply wrapped up and incinerated; there was no choice.

Our society is still singularly bad at dealing with death or allowing for the fact that the grieving process is a necessary part of carrying on with life . . . Feelings of grief in our culture (often quite frightening in their ferocity and variety) must be hidden away behind closed doors; until they burst out, unleashing all sorts of problems . . .

Whenever and however the death of a child occurs, it means shock and disbelief. It may mean regrets about decisions taken at the time; it may mean missed opportunities; it may mean guilt; it may mean anger. One thing is certain; it always means being scarred for the rest of your life.

Children born after the death of a brother or sister

Some parents choose to have further children after the death of a child. There may be a surprising sense of how the past death is somehow connected to the new birth. Feelings towards the new infant life may be complicated, by extremes of anxiety and fear, doubt and terror. This is normal, but can make the early weeks and months very fraught and may make bonding with the new baby extremely difficult.

The courage of parents who lose a newborn child

This can be breathtaking. I read the following story in the *Observer*. After a successful textbook labour, one couple very suddenly lost their firstborn baby, Owen. One moment the mother was holding her gorgeous newborn son – the next moment he was not breathing, and he could not be resuscitated. It was several weeks later, on hearing the results of the postmortem examination, that the parents learned that their baby's death was due to a bacterial infection (Group B streptococcus) that afflicts 700 newborns every year, 100 of whom die. This infection can cause brain damage to surviving babies. The condition is easily treatable, but there was not at the time a UK-wide policy for preventing it.

Had Owen's parents been aware of the condition, his death could have been prevented with antibiotics. His mother commented on our living in a pervasive culture where nobody talks about things going wrong and babies dying at birth. She feels strongly that governments need to publish guidelines so that hospitals are aware of this, and that then and only then can the system look after mothers. 'I want to help because that is something positive we can do for Owen,' said his mother. 'If just one more baby lives, it will have been worth it.' Taking courage to talk will spread knowledge, and most certainly save the lives of many babies. This is Owen's legacy and his parents' mission.

When it comes to commemorating their child, bereaved families are sometimes distressed by restrictions placed on their choice of memorial or inscription. Stories occur regularly of parents who have been thwarted by the limitations imposed by local parish priests, who have the authority to make judgements on the type of memorial allowed in churchyards on the grounds of overall aesthetics. Clergy have to attend to the practical application of diocesan regulations and, when managing graveyards, parish priests are required to take account of the 'big picture' (including historical and heritage considerations), as well as the personal desires of bereaved families. As in all professions, some clergy can be less imaginative and flexible than others, but in the majority of cases a wise and sympathetic cleric will help all involved to come to an agreeable solution.

Babies who die before and during birth

Nearly a third of pregnancies end before birth. The impact of this experience is underestimated because there is an almost unstated assumption that there is no parent/child relationship; after all, the loss is not uncommon (there's that word again), and the foetus/embryo was invisible and inside its mother's body. But in reality there are no significant differences between the grief responses of women losing wanted babies through miscarriage, stillbirth or neonatal death.

Assumptions of 'no grief' following miscarriage or abortion, whether chosen or otherwise, may be not much more than a tacit admission of ignorance (Dunn, 2000). I am unaware of any study following up mothers in this situation to find out how they are doing, or whether/how they are recovering. In 1945 the American poet Gwendolyn Brooks spoke profoundly in her poem 'The Mother':

Abortions will not let you forget.
You remember the children you got and did not get,
The small damp pulps with a little or with no hair;
The singers and workers that never handled the air.
You will never neglect or beat
Them, or silence or buy with a sweet.
You will never wind up the sucking thumb
Or scuttle off ghosts that come.
You will never leave them, controlling your luscious sigh,
Return for a snack of them, with gobbling mother-eye.
I have heard in the voices of the wind the voices of
My dim killed children.
I have contracted, I have eased
My dim dears at the breasts they could never suck.
I have said, Sweets, if I sinned, If I seized
Your luck
And your lives from your unfinished reach,
If I stole your birth and your names,
Your straight baby tears and your games,
Your stilted or your lovely loves, your tumults, your marriage,
Aches and your deaths,
If I poisoned the beginnings of your breaths,
Believe that even in my deliberateness I was not deliberate.
Though why should I whine,
Whine that the crime was other than mine?
Since anyhow you are dead.
Or rather or instead
You were never made.
But that, too, I am afraid
Is faulty. Oh, what shall I say, how is the truth to be said?
You were born, you had body, you died.
It's just that you never giggled or planned or cried.
Believe me, I loved you all.
Believe me, I knew you, though faintly, and I loved,
I loved you All.

Miscarried or stillborn babies may not have a social identity, or have officially 'existed' for others. For the parents, however, and especially the expectant mother, there will be already formed bonds of recognition and hope. Though the mother and father will have little to remember about the unlived life, parents expecting a much-wanted child will have a dream baby in mind, possibly already named, and invest a great deal in this vision to the degree that, if the baby doesn't survive, part of the very self feels lost.

Just over a generation ago, it was not possible to 'see' the growing infant. Today, the erroneous assumption that there is little relationship between parents and foetus is made redundant by the use of ultra-sound scanning of the womb, which allows parents to see and bond with the developing child very early on in the pregnancy, even to know the child's sex if they wish.

When a baby dies, other problems may crowd in on the mother especially, but also on the father. The parents are often young; this may be their first experience of death. A baby's death is always shocking, particularly if the mother was healthy during the pregnancy. Overwhelming guilt is not unusual – 'What did I do wrong?' 'Am I fit to be a parent at all?' Pregnancy is so intimate; obvious as it sounds, the mother has a unique relationship with the baby. Who else knows this little one as well as she? Her loss therefore can be entirely lonely. Although during my pregnancies I joked about feeling like a campground for aliens, and when closer to full term like a beached beluga, I remember calling Sean, my firstborn child, by his name from early on in the pregnancy. This was also the case with Caitlin. The 50:50 chance of being correct about gender was fortunate in our case.

It is important not to underestimate a mother's need for grieving her baby's death. If she is a solo expectant mother, she is too often truly on her own. Fathers who are involved in their partner's pregnancy are often reticent about expressing feelings and end up being entirely ignored. Like bereaved sisters and brothers (see Chapter 4), the father may set aside his own grief to look after the mother.

Feelings engendered by the above losses are also present even when the mother wishes to end the pregnancy – for example, when foetal abnormality leads the mother to choose abortion. Economic and emotional reasons for seeking to stop the pregnancy can have a much more complex effect than relief. Very often, there are feelings of self-hatred, self-blame and guilt over a baby who was wanted but whose birth seemed impossible.

I recall Emma, a talented 18-year-old student who came to me for help. In the middle of her final year at sixth form college she 'fell' pregnant to Tim, her 19-year-old boyfriend. Emma truly loved Tim, but she discovered that not long before she started going out with him, he had got another (15-year-old) girl pregnant. This girl was going ahead with her pregnancy. Unsurprisingly, Emma's relationship with Tim did not survive this information.

Emma's visit to her local GP was very painful. The doctor was offhand and disapproving and implied that Emma was probably one of the sort of girls who 'wouldn't even have second thoughts' after an abortion. Luckily for Emma she received careful and non-judgemental counselling from her parish priest and from a counsellor at the local hospital. Supported unconditionally by those who cared about her, Emma made the agonizing decision to end her pregnancy. She named the baby Benjamin, saying that she was certain the baby was a boy, and wanted him to know she loved him and that she was sorry. The health services required her to wait until she was three months' pregnant to have the abortion in the hospital day clinic. Up to the very last minute, Emma knew that what she felt to be the right decision in going through with the abortion was not what she wanted in her heart of hearts. I hope she has recovered from the self-blame she heaped on herself. Whatever your position on the issue of abortion, and this is not the place for debating the issue, it would be not only insensitive, but actually wrong, to say that Emma was nonchalant or ill-considering of the difficult choice she made.

Babies who become ill

The child addressed in the following letter is my god-daughter, Venice Caitlin McKeen. One day Venice's mother Ann Marie, a solo mother in her mid-twenties, noticed that 16-month-old Venice was fretful and, unusually for her, not interested in her food. The doctor found a distention of the abdomen which was confirmed in hospital as an abdominal neuroblastoma, a particularly aggressive and rare cancer in children over the age of one. Venice was admitted immediately to hospital and began a course of chemotherapy.

I visited Venice on the day her chemotherapy began. When I heard that her chances of surviving the cancer are not very optimistic – 20–25 per cent – I found the statistic most unhelpful in my attempts to create a strategy of hope for her survival tempered by realism. I decided to write Venice a letter to be opened on her sixteenth birthday. The letter is reprinted here:

18 July 2017

Happy birthday, Venice dear,

You are 'sweet sixteen'! In my mother's day they used to say 'sweet sixteen and never been kissed'. By the time I was a teenager myself, it was 'sweet sixteen and never been missed'!

As I write this, in the new year of 2003, you have been in the world now for less than two years. You were born beautiful, brown and bouncy, a thoroughly healthy baby girl.

I suppose that my writing you in this way may seem a strange thing for your godmother to do. But I came home from visiting you on a cold winter's night after your first chemotherapy treatment for the sudden cancer which attacked you like a cruel thief and felt I just had to do something *hopeful* for you.

I chose your sixteenth birthday because you were 16 months old when the cancer struck, and it's another '16', and this time hopefully a very lucky number. Sixteen years is 192 months, and 192 months is 5,844 days! Wow! Anyway, part of what happened to you was this. From nowhere, a bolt out of the blue, you became ill, very ill. The doctors used frightening words like 'neuroblast-oma', 'aggressive cancer', and 'serious cell involvement'.

They were asking your mum Ann Marie to sign forms and consent to procedures which sounded more dangerous than death itself and which no parent could imagine signing until faced with such a terrifying dilemma – the dilemma being this:

The doctors said, 'I'm sorry, Ms McKeen, but we must use very powerful toxic drugs which endanger Venice's life in an effort to save her life. There is no doubt that without intervention, she will die – we hope to be able to help Venice live.' So. Your mum, being the brave feisty type of woman she is, well, she took a good tough look at the situation, saw she was at the end of her tether, tied a knot in the tether and hung on for dear life, holding and hugging you all the way.

We so desperately hoped and prayed and loved you moment by

moment through this frightening illness. We knew, as you could not, that this was a vicious cancer and that there was no way of making things pretty. Scientists talk statistics and early on the one that caused nightmares was this one: you had a 20–25 per cent chance of growing up. The hardest thing at the time for everybody was not being able to explain to you why so many strangers were poking and prodding you about and giving you medicines that hurt. Again and again and again. After all, you were only 16 months old.

The chemotherapy treatment, which when it works destroys the nasty tumour in your stomach, made you feel absolutely terrible: nausea, sore mouth, difficulty swallowing, lost resistance to common ills like colds and pneumonia, disappeared appetite, difficulty sleeping through the night, difficulty staying awake . . . this list went on and on.

But do you know what? Through all the indignity and Hickman lines and nasal-gastric tubes, all the needles puncturing you like an inside-out hedgehog, you had some very good days, bouncing around the ward and around Grampy Mike's and Grammy Linda's house like a little tornado, grinning at everyone and terrorizing adult toes with your doll's pram. Give up? Not you! A permanent and delightful picture in my mind will be of you, attached to your chemotherapy drip stand on wheels, tearing down the hall in your ward, followed by your huggy-bear grandfather Mike weaving along in your wake, navigating the drip stand with the finesse of a prima ballerina.

Time turned inside out, and every moment was both a lifetime and a snapshot. When I visited you in hospital, it was at the time of your first dose of chemotherapy. After that, and in stages, you received five more injections of this chemical. The chemotherapy seemed such a blunt instrument to use, but was, as far as we knew at the time, the only treatment known to save your life. Then they operated and took away what was left of the tumour and you got through that seven-hour operation. And we would do everything in our power to save you. I want to let you know how much you were, and are, loved and how dearly you delight your mum Ann Marie, Grammy Linda and Grampy Mike. I want you to know how beautiful you were both then and now. How do I know you're still beautiful at 16? Because I am very very smart.

During these years between your illness and this special

birthday I've been saving a bit of money for you. Do whatever you want with it; put it into savings (boring!) – buy something beautiful to wear – or jewellery – treat yourself! You deserve it.

Love always from your godmother, Linda

PS Just remembered – it's my 75th birthday coming up in a couple of weeks, so let's pop the cork on a bottle of bubbly and celebrate. xx

As this book neared completion, Venice had responded very well to the treatment. Her tumour, once the size of a tennis ball, was reduced to the dimension of a marble. Surgeons had removed the tumour in a seven-hour operation, which was followed up with 'targeted radiotherapy' conducted on an out-patient basis. By mid-summer 2003 Venice's family and friends were looking for a recovery – and dared to say a 'cure'. All being well, from now on, Venice will be monitored regularly for as long as she lives. Neuroblastomas have a nasty habit of recurring. The hope of Venice's loved ones is, as it would be for all parents for their children, that it skips over Venice.

Venice's story is being replayed around the world when parents find that their much-loved and wanted healthy baby, in whom they invest all bright hopes, is blighted by the ravages of sudden disease.

Babies who live, and sick babies who have died

I don't know whether Venice will live or die, and I don't even know whether the letter for her sixteenth birthday will help her and her family. But I do know that it was something that would not hurt because it presumes hope, that Cinderella of the trinity of graces – faith, hope and love. My friend Mike ('Grampy' in the above letter) says that there are two main personality types in humans, the 'glass-half-full' and the 'glass-half-empty' sort. He says I'm a glass-half-full girl.

Faith, hope and love are enshrined as the 'big three' graces to make for an abundant life, with love topping the charts. But I'm not so sure about that. Love is so dangerous ('Grief is the price we pay for love,' said Colin Murray Parkes, the great bereavement guru), and faith is so controversial. Plus, many feel we are losers when it comes to love and faith. But hope?

When a baby dies, hope, along with delight and confidence, pride and faith in the future, seems shattered, snuffed out. How to make sense of such senseless loss? So it seemed and may yet seem. To hope again seems the most dangerous and perhaps fruitless act of all, but do you know anyone who is truly hopeless? Of the three qualities, I'm beginning to think hope should get the long straw.

John Cleese once memorably remarked, 'I can cope with despair; it's the hope I can't live with.' Hope isn't really the same as optimism, and does not even presuppose with any certainty that things will turn out well. Hope is a kind of assurance that something will make sense regardless of the outcome. This hope extends to all babies; *in vitro* babies who are aborted, either naturally or not, neonates who are born still, or live a few days or months, cot deaths, the lot.

Last century ('last century' meaning only a few years ago) an eminent man called Karl Menninger pointed out that our book-shelves are pretty bare when it comes to hope – unlike love and faith, he notes that poor little hope is often not even listed in reference books.

I'm referring of course, not to 'hope' the place, but to 'hope' as it 'springs eternal in the human heart' or, more darkly, in Dante's inscription over the entrance to hell: 'Abandon all hope, you who enter!'

I have noticed in conversations with fellow bereaved friends that the images preferred by those of us who have lost tiny babies/ younger children, and those whose older and adult children died, tend to be very different. Babies and young children conjure images of rainbows, butterflies, flowers, angels, fluffy clouds and blue skies. What is helpful in 'young child' images is the quality of hope and transformation that inhabits them. Is this hope possible in the first and following days/years of losing a baby? Probably not. Taking one breath at a time, one step at a time, we move into an unknown future, where we *hope* we can regain *hope*.

Even when our baby has been ill for some time and we know that s/he may not survive, we still haven't time to truly take in the import of death, should it happen. But something in the nature of living in the moment, those good days or hours or minutes of sheer love, may lift the pain to a level that allows us to accept that our children's lives, no matter the brevity, no matter how untimely, were not for nothing.

At one recent gathering for bereaved families a stark contrast in response to the loss of a baby came up between two couples in a group meeting. Both families were 'traditional' families – that is, married couples. Both had within the last year lost a baby. Both mothers were once again pregnant, and by nearly the same number of months. One little toddler, Kelly (I have changed names), tragically caught herself in a rotary clothesline and choked to death; her father Michael remains beside himself with grief because he had run into the house for something – no more than two minutes away at most – and on his return to the garden found his little girl. He was unable to resuscitate her. He and his wife Sandra did not plan the present pregnancy.

The other couple, Philip and Paula, lost their baby Alexandra at nine months of age to meningitis. After her death the couple organized and wrote a memorial celebration together of the baby's life. They clearly saw the present pregnancy as a tribute to Alexandra and an affirmation of the future.

Sandra and Michael were, however, terrified at the prospect of the new life they were nurturing. Clearly there was much forgiving of selves and facing the pregnancy to be done. But the problem arose in the discussion group when Sandra and Michael expressed their feeling that Philip and Paula were, in their opinion, smug about losing Alexandra. Philip and Paula went very quiet and then Philip looked Michael in the eye and said, 'I am so sorry for what all of us have gone through. I hope you will be able to forgive yourself enough to welcome your new baby.'

One clear message from this exchange bears repeating: *we are all unique in the way we grieve*. Our grieving personalities are made up of all our complex and unique life experiences. Not only are we different in the way we grieve our baby's death, but we will change over the years. In any group of, say, a dozen bereaved parents, there will be a dozen different ways of coping or bearing the loss. One of us can't stop eating, another can't take a bite. One keeps constantly busy, another sits and stares endlessly. One can't sleep, another can't stay awake. And so on. None of these ways are 'right' or 'wrong'. It is crucial not to judge the actions, motives, thoughts and beliefs of others.

Things not to say to those whose baby has died

- 'Just have another one.'
- 'You're looking well. Over it yet?'
- 'You'll soon get closure.'
- 'It's a blessing in disguise.' (This prize blooper is often specially reserved for those whose baby was disabled or suffered from a disease.)
- 'It's lucky you're young.'
- 'Be grateful you can have/already have other children.'
- 'It was God's will.'

Most bereaved parents will agree that saying nothing would be better than these statements. 'I cannot imagine how you must be feeling' would be far preferable. Or try, 'I'm so sorry.' Or a hug.

Frances Dominica is an Anglican nun who founded Helen House in Oxford, the world's first hospice for children with life-limiting illnesses and their families. In her book *Just My Reflection: Helping Parents to Do Things Their Way When Their Child Dies* (Dominica, 1997), she writes:

Saying to parents whose child has died, 'You will get over it', is like saying, 'One day it will seem as if he never existed.' Nothing could be more hurtful. They don't want him [sic] written out of existence. But given time, given permission to be who they are, given reassurance to behave instinctively, given love and friendship, I believe that they will have the best chance to adjust to what has happened and grow towards healing and wholeness. Despite society's fear of death and ineptitude in the face of death, I believe that every individual has the potential within to meet death with a severe beauty which in no way denies grief. Being alongside such families you absorb some of their grief. But you also share some of the good things:

- learning to think of time in terms of depth rather than length;
- enjoying the swift growth of real friendship;
- bypassing the usual obstacles of class, creed, colour, age, education;
- having 'all one's sensitivities heightened' as one father put it.

And you begin to reverence the nobility and beauty in every man, woman, and child because tragedy lifts the mask of pretence and truth is revealed.

I conclude this chapter with lyrics written by Karen Taylor Good:

Precious child

In my dreams you are alive and well,
Precious child, precious child.
In my mind I see you clear as a bell,
Precious child, precious child.

In my soul there is a hole
That can never be filled,
But in my heart there is hope
Because you are with me still.

In my heart you live on,
Always there, never gone,
Precious child, you left too soon.
Though it may be true that we're apart,
You will live forever in my heart.

In my plans I was the first to leave,
Precious child, precious child.
But in this world I was left here to grieve,
Precious child, my precious child.

In my soul there is a hole
That can never be filled,
But in my heart there is hope
And you are with me still.

In my heart you live on,
Always there, never gone,
Precious child, you left too soon.
Though it may be true that we're apart,
You will live forever in my heart.

God knows I want to hold you,
See you, touch you,

And maybe there's a heaven
And some day I will again.
Please know you're not forgotten until then.

In my heart you live on,
Always there, never gone,
Precious child, you left too soon.
Though it may be true that we're apart,
You will live forever . . . in my heart.

4

Sisters and Brothers

When you died I felt like I had been hit by a plank. I could barely stand up, much less walk. I kept losing my balance and bumping into walls. Right now I am learning to walk again. One day I hope I can fly.

> (Amy Eldon, to her brother Dan, who was murdered)

Not many months after Caitlin's death I was sitting quietly with friends on the lawn outside Gloucester Cathedral when a young child skipped straight up to me, plopped herself by my side and smiled as glowingly at me as if I were a favourite auntie. I'd never seen her before.

'Hi there,' I said. 'Where's your mummy?'

'Over there,' she nodded vaguely over her shoulder. I couldn't see anyone. I offered her a crisp which she took and nibbled. 'Have you any brothers and sisters?'

'Yep. One in heaven and one in Basingstoke. Bye!'

She was away as quickly as she had arrived. My eyes followed her skipping form to the person I presume to have been her mother.

Since then, I have got round the thorny problem of meeting new people who ask those occasional questions that tear at the heart of bereaved brothers, sisters and parents – 'Have you any children/ sisters/brothers?' Now I might quite likely say, 'Yes. I've two children. One in heaven and one in Deptford,' which is where my son lives.

William Wordsworth captured the tenacious tie between siblings:

> 'How many are you,' then said I,
> 'If they two are in heaven?'
> Quick was the little maid's reply,
> 'O Master, we are seven.'
> 'But they are dead; those two are dead!
> Their spirits are in heaven!'
> 'Twas throwing words away; for still
> The little maid would have her will,
> And said, 'Nay, we are seven!'

74

Nearly half of all children under 18 in England and Wales are not being brought up in a 'traditional' family – that is, with their parents married and living together under the same roof (Office of National Statistics, Census 2001). Large numbers live in lone-parent families, most commonly headed by the mother, and in stepfamilies with a remarried parent. Many more are brought up by unmarried cohabiting couples, both heterosexual and homosexual. The trend away from conventional marriage continues, and there are clearly problems specific to bereaved step-siblings (as opposed to blood-related and adopted siblings) that deserve further study.

Explaining the situation to young children

It is extremely difficult to find a way of explaining death to young children, although it is our adult use of language rather than their innate resilience that is more often the problem. We find that there are quite simply 'no words' to fit the immensity of what has happened. As I mentioned earlier, my own mother, Rosalie, died of Hodgkin's disease when I was six years old. I was never told that she was seriously ill, and when she died my father took me aside into a little room in Auntie Ruth's house to say through his tears that 'Mom is very happy now. She's in heaven.' So I didn't cry, and wandered back to the living room into a heaving mass of sobbing adult relatives. I remember saying, 'Why is everybody crying? You're supposed to be happy.' Had my mother been my brother or sister, I daresay my response would have been identical.

My older brother Roy, the eldest of the three of us, was allowed to go to our mother's funeral, but my sister Nancy, who is three years my senior, and I were not permitted to attend. We showed our anger at being excluded by placing a Monopoly board on the floor directly in line with the front door of the house, thus requiring the lucky mourners allowed to attend the funeral to step over or walk around us, which they did. Nobody asked us to move the Monopoly board.

Fortunately, things have changed since the mid-twentieth century and parents today would be less likely to stop children going to a close relative's funeral without very good reason. I filled the huge vacuum in life left by my mother's death by believing fervently that night-times, when she came to me in my dreams, were truly real, and that daytime, the dull regimen of school and meals and routines dictated by governesses and housekeepers, were dreams. Fortu-nately, I never informed the grown-ups of this aberrant thinking. I say 'fortunate', because in retrospect I believe that I might have been exposed to less-than-helpful therapy or medication that would have killed my mother yet again, metaphorically speaking. This reversal of day and night continued for some time, and I wonder if attending the funeral would have provided some way of bidding farewell to Mother, who had been my everything. As it is, we're still saying 'hello'. Perhaps not such a terrible thing.

A child aged under four is unlikely to comprehend explanations, and yet studies reveal the deep effect that a sibling's death has, even on the very young. In her landmark book *The Bereaved Parent* (Schiff, 1999), Harriet Sarnoff Schiff tells of the time she tried to explain the death of her daughter's older brother to four-year-old Stacie:

> I began by simply saying Robby was dead. She asked, 'For how long will he be dead?' I replied, 'Forever. He will never be back.' But a four-year-old, no matter how astute, just cannot grasp 'forever'. I could see how puzzled and frightened she was. She asked what happens when a person dies. And here I used extreme care, consciously avoiding the dangerous pitfall of saying 'he went to sleep'. I believe such a statement could induce a fear of sleep that could last forever. Instead, I said he stopped breathing . . . Then came the toughie.
> 'Why?'
> I began by saying he was very sick and she countered that she had been sick many times. I said Robby was a different kind of sick.

Stacie kept asking why. Finally her mother told her an untruth: that Robby was hurting. 'Something she could understand. After that, the "Why" stopped.'

Sarnoff Schiff's suggestions to parents wanting to help surviving children bear repeating:

- Continue normal patterns of discipline. This will be reassuring – the old 'boundaries' thing.
- Try to discover early on if there are 'my fault' feelings about the death.
- Remind the sister or brother of nice things they did – there are always nice things.

- Explain that arguments and jealousy are totally natural.
- Explain that wishing the brother/sister were dead is also normal and that wishing doesn't 'create a dead person'.
- Don't say it was God's will. It won't help.
- Expect the children to laugh and play earlier than you expect.
- Don't pressurize children to go to the cemetery.
- It is natural to idealize your dead child. Try not to turn her/him into a plaster saint. None of us can compete with a perfect dead person.
- Your children suffer just as you suffer. The power of these feelings can be terrifying for them too.
- Try to explain that death is a mystery to all of us, and that we can't really control it.
- Keep talking about the dead child. Trying to shut out the pain by shutting up won't work.
- Don't hide grown-up grief. Encourage your children to express theirs too. Grief isn't just for sissies, girls and mothers.
- Sometimes, this death may be the first time children have seen their father cry. Men are often still taught to withhold emotion, but this can be easily misinterpreted by children as aloofness or not caring. Children can see that men feel pain and cry too. It's not just for girls and mothers. Boys and fathers can show how awful they feel too.

Is there a way to avoid the general impression felt by Schiff that 'no one remembered a positive interplay with parents during the grieving period'? I imagine that it is never too late to open the subject up, however difficult, discussing mistakes honestly and trying to resolve them.

Young children are often susceptible to mishearing remarks and taking them entirely to heart. I clearly remember overhearing something said by my beloved grandmother not long after my mother Rosalie died. Mama Morris said, 'You know, Rosalie had been ill ever since Linda was born.' I interpreted this to mean that my birth caused my mother's incurable cancer, a conviction that festered away quietly until I reached my teens.

At one bereavement group a sibling counsellor gave the following guidelines, making the point that age divisions are flexible and that she hoped she wouldn't sound patronizing to parents who would know their own child better than anyone else.

- Babies and toddlers may not have words yet, but research shows that they are deeply affected by their parents' emotions and by the atmosphere around them. Grief does affect babies in long-term ways too, not just in disruption of breastfeeding or different carers; babies absorb the distress and it often shows in disrupted sleep, changes in appetite, increased crying. Help is largely through physical security, hugging even through the tears, letting the infant share a room or bed for a while. A child is never too young to be affected by death and loss.
- Before the age of five it may be difficult for a child to understand that death is final. Answer questions that come, and no more. Be minimalist. It's an individual matter whether to include God in the conversation – if you do, best not blame God. Be prepared to repeat the facts many times. Try not to be upset if, two minutes into a heartfelt discussion, the child asks if they can 'go and watch telly now'. Follow the child's timetable.
- In early years, children see themselves as the centre of the family world, and the trauma of death can be both shattering and confusing. They may believe that they can do magic, and by being good can bring back their dead sibling. They may also fear that they caused the death somehow.

Children of junior school age are often at a stage of curiosity about death, and interested in grisly details. They may be fascinated by physical details of the death and what happens to the body, including very specific questions about burial or cremation. They begin to have a personal view about death, that it will one day happen to others that they love and to them, which can lead to a deep concern for people who are sick or old.

I recall burying a baby mockingbird I'd been unable to save. I put it in a tightly taped waterproof box, buried it, and dug it up a month later. It was at this time I used to go round chanting with my friends:

> Did you ever think that by and by that someday you're going to die,
> Har-umph, Har-umph, Har-umph, Har-umph, Har-umph!
> They'll cover you up with a big white sheet
> And dig you a hole about sixty feet deep, Har-umph, etc.
> The worms crawl in, the worms crawl out,
> The worms play pinochle on your snout,

They eat your eyes, they eat your nose,
They eat the jelly between your toes . . .

I think this was a song we didn't sing to the grown-ups – hardly a mature meditation on dead bodies, but it had a certain macabre fascination. The lyrics both describe and demonize death and decomposition, and though I don't remember ever thinking of death as monstrous, it is easy to see how many children would see it as an evil devouring thing that snatches us away. The important thing is reassurance; and don't be put off if children return our attempts at loving reassurance with distance or even hostility. Some children are better at vicarious mourning, finding it easier to empathize with fictional characters in books or on television than their own brother or sister. Be ready for over-reactions too. A lost toy thought by us parents to have been long forgotten can be the source of huge distress.

Many children fear their own death, and fear losing their parents. Roy, my older brother, told us that Mom looked 'peaceful just like she was asleep'; this description did not help my sleep patterns. Ask children what they are afraid of. An accidental mishearing can cause internal havoc – for example, hearing the word 'lost' can be interpreted as lost and found, prompting a search for the lost sibling. If a sister or brother died in hospital, it may be thought that the hospital killed her or him.

Play

At all stages, play is crucial to understanding what has happened. Children may act out a sibling's death with toys; they may encourage friends to play games in which killing and dying are what happens. It is important that parents notify the playgroup or school of the family death, and hopefully speak to the surviving child's teacher. Sometimes children can express themselves eloquently through drawing, painting, clay or Plasticine when they are unable to find words. Violent, dark feelings will be more manageable if there's not a need to explain them.

The behaviour of children of all ages may regress – they may have sleep problems, bedwetting, bursts of rage; out of the blue they may become very aggressive. They may become extremely clingy and dependent, or take up thumb-sucking again. Family resources are taxed to the limit – the key is maintaining previous family boundaries with a lot of closeness and loving and holding (Schiff, 1999).

The body of the child who has died is no longer doing what bodies do; it cannot breathe or touch or move, and it cannot be woken up. 'Brother/Sister' is not just asleep. The body has completely stopped working and cannot wake up. Some children, on being told that the body looks peaceful, just like when sleeping, become fearful of going to sleep. It is vital to make sure that the child knows the difference between death and sleep, for otherwise at the funeral or cremation the child can be terrified by thinking that her brother/sister might be hurting. If it is appropriate to view the body, many parents find it helpful to let children see their dead brother or sister. They will be able to see that the living person is just not there.

Should young children go to funerals?

Should very young children go to the funeral of a dead brother or sister? The answer, I repeat, is yes in most cases, not least because I have heard endless stories from years later of bitterness and resentment at exclusion. Little ones may fidget, or play distracting games at the funeral. Older sisters and brothers may find the funeral silly or even phoney, and may hate going to the cemetery the way the adults do.

Bereavement experts differ over this one. Some advise not taking a child younger than seven to the funeral – however, I still believe firmly that both my sister and I, aged nine and six when my mother died, should have been allowed to go to the funeral. To my mind, having taken in the fact that my mother wasn't coming back, it would have been a good idea to allow me to say goodbye. The same would hold true when a brother or sister dies.

At Caitlin's funeral we anticipated there would be a number of young children, so we brought her very beautiful rocking horse to the church and placed it in front of the pulpit. At home the rocking horse, named 'I Dare You' by Caitlin, is a focal point of our home. It was a gift from me for her second birthday and virtually every child who comes through our front door heads straight for a ride on I Dare You.

I'd go further than recommending children's inclusion in the funeral. If time permits, try to include them in planning as well. The idea of taking the rocking horse to the church came from a five-year-old, and the idea of placing the basket of letters from Caitlin's child friends in the grave with her coffin was the idea of another child. After the funeral, ask for surviving children's views on how you will deal with special occasions, birthdays, holidays, etc., and get their thoughts about plans for their sibling's room and clothes. Inclusion is very important.

Older siblings

Siblings, especially older brothers and sisters, may not feel the overwhelming powerlessness that parents feel. They may forget good things and remember things that make them feel guilty, and dwell on arguments and teasing and bad feelings. In the rough and tumble of sibling rivalry, punching and furious rows can overwhelm the good memories – the tattling, beating up, the teasing to enrage.

Taking the blame for imaginary scenarios can happen. Jealousy over changes in affection can lead a child to think, 'She's dead because I was jealous that she got a boyfriend and wouldn't let me tag along. She just closed me out of her life and called me a baby. Then she had the accident and died. God is punishing me for being jealous.'

Most parents from a faith tradition will remain people of faith however tested the tenets of their belief system are by the loss of their child. There's a jargon for this phenomenon, called 'personality intensification', which simply means that, as we grow older, most of us get more like we've always been, despite the suffering we have endured. Siblings often ask the same questions that parents ask, but may well be much more deeply shaken:

- 'If God is God, he's not good if he let my sister die.'
- 'I believe there's a God, but I don't think you should trust him very much.'
- 'I prayed and prayed to save him, but he died anyway. I don't pray any more. Who cares about the afterlife? I need him now.'

Parental explanations – 'She is at peace now', 'It was God's will', 'Now he belongs to the angels' – may be unhelpful to siblings. The

'God's will' statement can lead one to conclude that God made a terrible mistake and was to blame, and was picking on 'my brother', 'my sister'. Home can come to represent sadness rather than sanctuary, and older siblings may well want to be away from the awful pall of emptiness. House equals death, especially if their sibling died at home. They may want to spend virtually all free time with friends, believing that Mum and Dad are 'just hopeless'.

I write primarily from the perspective of a bereaved parent, not a sibling. Although I have done my homework, I also feel very much my limitations in addressing the issue of older bereaved brothers and sisters; the more research, the less confidence. What I have gleaned from my own son and from countless siblings reveals that understanding can take me only so far. In addition, what seems important in the 'big picture' is quite simply to try and be present for the best and worst of everything. I can, of course, support him/them at all times when needed, but I cannot take the burden of their own grief from them. And it is difficult to overstate that support is made difficult by the fact that we parents are going through the most soul-destroying experience of our lives.

To brothers and sisters it is the emptiness of losing someone of one's own generation. Sometimes the lost sibling can be the first experience of death. All the shared stuff of life, even shared conflicts and arguments, are gone for ever. Parents will try to fill this void, but may be the least qualified to do so, because we have lost someone we expected and hoped to outlive us.

Parents will need to draw upon every reserve to meet the children's need for us to listen and talk and attend to them at a time when just functioning is at a all-time low.

So just what can mothering and fathering be expected to be at this time? The brother/sister relationship has been severed. Again and again the testimonies of surviving siblings show that at the time of the death of their brother or sister they felt totally alone.

Even at a very young age, children may feel the need to protect their parents. Pat Neil, my predecessor as editor of TCF's quarterly journal, learned some years after her son Ruairidh's death that his younger sibling Sandy, barely seven years old, had suggested to older sister Lisa that they 'should not worry or trouble Mum and Dad' while things were so bad. Pat felt distressed, 'that this small person had been looking out for me so carefully, and I had been doing hardly anything for him, as I know now, although I thought I was making a reasonable fist of it at the time ... So I think that protective thing starts very early on indeed – depending of course on how observant and thoughtful the child is by nature. Some are, some aren't.'

Ask the parents even years later and they will say that they tried their best to console and care for surviving siblings, and that often this maximum effort was the only effort they were able to make at the time. Which, I am afraid, may end up being another version of 'damned if we do, damned if we don't'. On balance, though, the 'do' is better than the 'not do'. If we parents are to be of help to our surviving children at this time, we need first to think through our own understanding of death, and then to think about our children's often very different understanding of death. Talk the talk, walk the walk.

In spite of having a more mature grasp of what is happening, older siblings are sometimes difficult to help, and may well feel that it is the parents who are creating and perpetuating the difficulties. They are often likely to be most at ease with friends instead of parents. All the normal facets of growing to young adulthood – conflicting emotions, hormones running wild, trying to reach a point of 'flying the nest' – can get in the way of helpful communication. Teens and young adults tend to be acutely aware of issues of life and death; and adult behaviour in the public arena – for example, seeing an adult world incapable of conducting its affairs and settling disputes without going to war – can lead to a questioning of the meaning of life in the light of their understanding. The death from whatever cause of a brother or sister leaves a deep and profound mark. Older siblings may feel guilty for still being alive and suffer survivor guilt – 'It should have been me' – and feel powerless in the face of family grief. Sometimes siblings will indeed need to find a way of forgiving or asking forgiveness from their dead sister or brother for hurtful things said or done in the past, but that still cause pain.

Most bereaved young people feel a terrific responsibility for their parents and sometimes try to be two people, replacing their sister or brother as well as being themselves. Or there may well be difficulties with the dead child whose virtues are extolled and whose less attractive qualities are forgotten. This can happen just at the time when surviving siblings are aware that they are behaving in an unacceptable way that it is difficult for them to do anything about.

Surviving children often feel they must become 'virtual parents' themselves. If this protectiveness is at the expense of coping with their own grief, it can be a time bomb waiting to explode in difficulties later on. Friends too often compound the problem with the well-meaning but mistaken belief that by saying things like, 'Look after your mum' or 'How's Dad coping?', they are bolstering up the surviving sibling's importance. The urge to scream, 'What about ME?' can be overwhelming.

With all these unhappy and unconscious pressures, it isn't unusual for behaviour to change – and unfortunately not always for the better – after the death of a brother or sister. Parental authority just ain't what it used to be, and young adults in our culture are subjected via the media to huge pressures from all directions; in early bereavement especially, they are extremely vulnerable. Commercial interests compete for attention. Producers of powerful and addictive substances, both legal and illegal, ranging from Ecstasy and cannabis to alcohol and psychotropic drugs, target certain age groups as valuable customers. If this is the case in normal situations, it is exponentially so for grieving youngsters. Young people are encouraged to experiment with the trappings of adult life at ever younger ages, and often long before they are equipped to take on the emotional implications of a very unstable world out there. A first-time shuffle through some of the teen magazines will be an eye-opener for many parents – articles about 'blow jobs' and 'sex positions of the month' are commonplace reading in magazines aimed at girls in their early teens. We've spent more than a century inventing childhood like a marketable Aunt Sally, only to knock her over again and yet again with sex-obsessed nonsense.

There are no pat answers. Some siblings become over-productive, while others 'drop out'. Sometimes older siblings turn to very destructive behaviours – truancy, vandalism, alcohol and drug abuse – risking long-term damage to themselves. It is hard to keep channels of communication open at these times. I learned through personal experience that as Sean's mother I was the last person to be able to say to my distraught son that I understood his pain and would be here for him always. I also tried talking about how I wish I could have done what was needed more, but didn't know what to do. I explained that I love him just as much as I loved his younger sister, but attempts at communication were too often a minefield, and at times I felt that every well-meant remark hit a cul-de-sac of silence or deferral. In the end I was sidelined and probably rightly so. As an adult, my son has his own life and circle of friends. One can only hope that his choice of friends is as excellent as it was when he was a young boy.

We think of the teen years and young adult years as often being times of alienation and seeking peer acceptance as part of finding adult identity. Young adults who have lost a sibling almost universally feel 'different' from their friends, that they no longer fit in anywhere. And very very often, the complaint arises that although they were worried about their parent/s, they were also resentful of the fact that they were seldom asked how *they* were doing. Linda Camper, a bereaved teen sibling, writes:

'How is your mom doing?'
Is the basic question asked.
Sometimes an inquiry about Dad.
But so sadly seldom,
They do not ask the siblings.
They must be so sad.

True, the depth of parents' awful loss
Brings agony and pain.
But the children, the dear children
Really do hurt again and again.

They lost a brother or a sis
Their pain is just as real
Frustration, anger and fear
They, too, go through such hell.

Who is there to comfort them
To give a word of care
Everyone is more concerned
About the parents' welfare.

While the siblings
Drown in their hurt and pain
No one to hold them near
And let them know they are not to blame.
To uplift and ease their minds from fear.

Ben Sieff, whose older brother was murdered when Ben was 16, has given parents some memorable advice which is also applicable to his contemporaries (Sieff, 2003):

> Allow a teen to be a teen. Not only has their loss been difficult for them to get through, but they are also getting bombarded with all kinds of other stress. Never allow yourself to compare your surviving teen with the one who died. In my house, we had a bookshelf dedicated to the 'greatness' of my brother. One of the things that really angered me was that his memory was being distorted. He was a great brother, but he was no angel. I wanted to remember him for exactly who he was – good and bad included. One of the most important things that a grieving teen can have is a friend they can talk to. As a parent, this may be you, but more often it is not. There are several reasons for this. The teen may feel that bringing up the subject will only make the parent feel worse. One sibling called this 'parenting the parent'.

Most grievers, parents and children alike, inevitably tend to be very selfish. Parents may unwittingly feel that they are entitled to the most grief. Grief should not be competitive. In the main, parents who give a teen and older sibling a chance to express grief will see the sensitivity returned generously.

Bereaved sisters and brothers of all ages know that their parents need all the help they can get. Parents need, in turn, to learn to re-build new relationships with their children, and sometimes to re-channel the love of the dead child to those who are alive. This is not easy, and saying it's not easy is an understatement. There is still, though, much we can do to support our children, and most of it is simple and practical.

Practical ideas from a parental perspective to help surviving children

- Be honest. Try not to say anything the child will find out to be untrue, because lies are a recipe for distrust. On the other hand, don't 'build a skyscraper if they ask about a small tent' – in other words, don't supply too much information.
- Speak as far as possible at the child's level of understanding. Very young children will ask the same questions over and over. They

need this repetition not least because the concept of time is difficult to grasp, and words like 'for ever', 'always' and 'never' are impossible for them to grasp, even though these are the only words to explain what has happened.

- Don't hide either your grief or your insights. Trying to shield children from distress is a mistake. They are already upset, and children know when grown-ups are keeping secrets and feel insecure if they believe they are being shut out for whatever reason. This is a time for hugging and crying and holding on to one another for dear life. For dear life. Children will also need time away from parents, alone with their own thoughts, and with their friends. A bit of distance from parents will be no bad thing.

- To say 'I don't know' is not a crime. This is not a time for presenting our child with a copy of the *Bhagavad Gita* or the *Tibetan Book of the Dead*, or any new or previously unexplored system of beliefs.

- Children will hear many different stories about death. Skipping and hopping to school we used to say, 'If you step on a crack you'll break your mother's back', and truly wonder if we had this dangerous power. We used to change the name from 'mother' to whoever was on our 'hit list' at the time, but I do remember wondering if I had made my mother ill.

The physical shock of grief can leave us chilled to the very marrow and this is true for our children too, so comfort foods and favourite objects can be helpful. Some children stop eating and feel full up, while others eat more as if they are trying to fill an empty hole with food. Invite them to help you plan meals and help to cook them. By feeding emotional hunger we are fed, and soft cuddly warm clothes help children to feel safe and protected from harm. Grief is exhausting. Encourage a cuddle during the day if this is possible. You could keep a blanket or sleeping bag and pillow in the living room to encourage a short rest. This is even more important at night, and simple things like an extra blanket, a hot water bottle and a warm drink are a good idea. Nightlights, sweet music to listen to, leaving the door open, staying with them until they fall asleep, all help – along with loads of extra cuddles and words of reassurance. Don't forget treats and outings too. A walk to the park or a bit of kicking a ball around helps children to know that it's OK not to be sad all the time. Friends will help with this aspect too.

Loneliness can be a pitfall, especially if there were two children and now there is only one. If children have shared a room, it is hard to face an empty bedroom, and may be too much to cope with. Perhaps the children were quite close in age and did many things together, like going to school, visiting aunties or Gran. Whether they squabbled and fought is neither here nor there. There may be a good time to cuddle up and say how strange and sad you feel not to see them together any more.

Children and anger

A rule of thumb is that suppressing or bottling up emotions sets an emotional time bomb ticking away. Anger is just one difficult feeling. In fact, it can be very frightening. We all know the destructive capacity of anger and often teach our children that it is bad. We punish them for tantrums and tell them to 'get a grip', to control themselves, but in reality anger is an often necessary part of grief and loss. A child experiences anger as a surge of energy, expressed physically: through the mouth, in biting, screaming, swearing and spitting; through the hands, in pinching, punching, breaking, scratching; and through the feet, in kicking, stamping, running away. We can help to channel this rage: kicking a ball instead of kicking Mum; thumping a cushion or hammering a piece of wood, or tearing up a cardboard box instead of the favourite story book; encouraging running in the park, but not in the traffic. Of course, this is not easy in the midst of parental grief, but we do not help our children to grieve if they never see that we too are distressed and needing to cry. This is truly a balancing act. Siblings need to be clear that the death was not their fault.

Nightmares

Sometimes children may be afraid to go to sleep because of bad dreams, though it is true that night-time terrors, fears and imaginings are almost always worse than reality. For them, as for us, there is also the knowledge that falling asleep means waking up again to a world where we recall what has happened. When parental distress levels are on stalks, we try to protect the children from the worst of our grieving, doing a good deal of weeping and talking after we think they are asleep. But don't count on them being asleep. Let them in on comings and goings in the house – it's a good idea to let them know if you are expecting friends to visit, so they don't imagine secrets from which they are barred.

Love

The crucial point at such a time of new grieving is to continue being a parent to surviving offspring. Easy to say, and extremely hard to execute; it will call on every ravaged resource available to bereaved parents. And love. We love, knowing that it is risky, that the price of love is too often loss. Why do we love so much? As a Christian by persuasion, I believe we were made in God's image to love. If a faith position is not yours, replace the word 'God' with 'goodness' and love still emerges trumps. 'Do you want me to tell you something really subversive?' says Erica Jong. 'Love is everything it's cracked up to be. That's why people are so cynical about it . . . It really is worth fighting for, being brave for, risking everything for. And the trouble is, if you don't risk anything, you risk even more.'

As with Pat Neil's young son Sandy, who survived the sudden death of his brother Ruairidh, many bereaved children are also likely to feel obligated to comfort parents, and this instinct is often underlined when well-meaning friends ask after the parents and remind the surviving child/children to 'look after Mum and Dad' (see pages 84 and 85). Seeing parents weak and powerless may well bring out the protective side of older children too. Or they might turn away and say, 'I'm going to my room, or to Daisy's house.' Try to understand if your child wishes not to confide in you, but instead in their friends of a similar age; this can be especially likely with older siblings who may have lost their closest confidant when the brother/ sister died.

Long-term resentments can be allayed or prevented by reaching out to surviving children at this time. How we find the resources to do so will depend on our own support systems, whether we are going through this with a partner's support or dealing with this loss on our own. We teach our children to play by the rules, to observe boundaries, not to cheat. To be fair. The death of a sister or brother brings home the truth that not everything in life *is* fair. It is natural to idealize someone who has died, although if the siblings have had a combative time together, resentments can build after the death. You cannot compete with a dead brother or sister, and may feel quite miffed that your sibling is being 'shined up and polished and enshrined' after death. And if this shiny view is true, how can you possibly live up to it?

It bears repeating that what we think about death is important. We live in a society that largely avoids the universal fact of life's ending as a normal event, much less the totally out-of-joint death of a child; this can mean that, unless they have gone through the death of a pet or friend or an older member of the family, our children's only exposure to death may be through cartoons or computer games with toy guns, or films, or a friend who says, 'My Uncle George has just gone to heaven.' These exposures simply do not relate to the road crash that killed their sister, or the baby brother being fine one day and dead the next after a cot-death. It is always true to reply to a question like, 'Where has he gone?' with, 'I don't know exactly because I've not been dead.' But if we have beliefs, now is the time to share them with our children. In their own time, and in their own way, they will work out their own beliefs about life after life's end.

Bibliotherapy

Children can be remarkably buoyant in the face of bereavement, but unresolved childhood grief can reappear in emotional, behavioural or social problems years after the bereavement (Jones, 2001). Adults who as children were excluded from family and communal mourning when a death took place may be particularly vulnerable when bereaved in later life (Ainsworth-Smith, 2002). Children's bereavement programmes, however well-meaning and important, are not always the answer, and counselling some bereaved children can be less helpful than we would wish. Which is where bibliotherapy steps in. Not a recent concept, bibliotherapy (literally 'book-healing') is the practice of using books and stories as part of problem-solving – in our case, the problem being the death of a loved sister/brother.

Books and poems that deal thoughtfully with sibling death can be very helpful. Nature stories of dragonflies and butterflies, as well as books written from a religious perspective, can be a way of looking at complex questions of existence from a safe distance. This is because:

- Books can help us to understand feelings.
- Readers can identify with characters in books whose feelings are similar.
- Books can help readers become sensitive to the feelings of others.

The following organizations may be helpful in finding the best book for you or your loved one (more details are given in Helpful Contacts at the back of the book):

- The Compassionate Friends National Postal Library.
- CRUSE Bereavement Care (lists with basic reviews are available on request).
- MEDITEC Medical and Nursing (Mail Order Books). (A comprehensive catalogue on all medical aspects is available on request.)
- The Young Book Trust Library. The Children's Library at Young Book Trust receives a copy of every children's book published in the United Kingdom. All books are listed on a database with full bibliographic data, enabling books on any topic to be supplied on request. *YBT* (*Young Book Trust*) – published each term – produces a selection list of books reviewed by children.

Death does not destroy the place of the lost brother or sister in the family, and it is a truism that the only thing worse than speaking ill of the dead is not speaking of them at all. They live in our memories and in our hearts, and we can talk about them with love and affection, remembering the mischievous and outright naughty, along with the sweet.

I corresponded with one teenager, Katy, who observed that when her brother died, she lost her parents too. 'Two things were clear pretty soon after Kevin died,' she said. 'I lost Kevin to his death, and I lost my mum and dad to their grief.' From the time at the hospital when her mother fainted into Katy's father's arms at the news that her child could not be saved, and then when her father collapsed, Katy was 'put in charge', first by the nurse who handed her brother's belongings to her in a plastic bag, and then when she drove her parents home and put them to bed.

Katy realized that her parents were not in a position to help her with her own grief, but she was also aware that she needed someone to help her. Her initial solution was to push all her feelings away, and 'not think about Kevin's death'. Friends and family did ask how she was, and her answer was 'fine'. She said 'fine' because she discovered pretty early on that nobody really wanted to hear, or perhaps could not bear to hear, the whole truth. Least of all her parents, who scarcely could deal with their own grief.

After a time, Katy's parents encouraged her to attend a SIBBS (Support in Bereavement for Brothers and Sisters) meeting at her local chapter of The Compassionate Friends, which she resisted at first, but now says was her first step in healing. Katy did not have high expectations of the group, and so was quite surprised to discover that the meetings were beneficial. She found people who uniquely had the vocabulary to deal with her feelings; and from now on, she decided, she would be leading a different life, no going back. She discovered importantly that feelings she thought were unique to her ('I feel so alone') were universal in her group.

It is now some years since her brother's death, and Katy knows that she has a completely different outlook on life. Life is very precious, and she values time more consciously. She feels closer to her parents and handles stress by 'chilling', though she does feel obligated to 'live life 100 per cent better in Kevin's memory'. And to be a 'better human being' – 'I quite like being a goody two shoes!' she joked. 'Kevin would fall about laughing if he were here. He was such a hell-raiser!'

Another girl lost her older brother when she was seven, but it was only many years later that she could articulate what she had felt at the time. First she was scared because Mummy and Daddy were so sad. She recalled that on the day of her brother's funeral a relative took her aside and told her to be very brave and try not to cry in front of her parents. She thought that if she tried to do the kind of things her brother had done – playing football and learning the guitar – that this might help; she became very proficient at both, even better than her adored big brother, and then felt guilty because she *was* better. Loss and grief are part of life for us all, even young children. This particular child did not need protection from loss as much as she needed the support of loving adults. So many children feel compelled to protect their parents, and this is probably not possible.

Amy

When it comes to 'top-flight sisters', Amy Eldon is right there at the pinnacle. She enjoyed an international and privileged upbringing:

I was brought up in Kenya, England and America, where the international school I attended shaped my worldview like nothing else in my childhood. Because everyone was from a different background, we could ignore external differences and focus on the individual. What you looked like didn't really matter. We all felt connected, part of the same tribe.

I taught Amy at the American School in London, and met her gifted mother Kathy at a parent-teacher meeting; we lunched a couple of times and enjoyed chatting about projects and life in general. After Amy graduated and I moved to the country, we kept in touch from time to time. Then I heard that a family tragedy had occurred, and contacted the Eldons. Amy's older and only brother – Dan – had been murdered.

Dan was a talented young photographer on placement with Reuters in Somalia, but on 12 July 1993 he was stoned to death, along with three other journalists. The attack was random retribution by an angry mob reacting to a UN bombing raid on the suspected headquarters of General Mohammed Farah Aidid. In a moment of hideous irony, Dan and his friends were murdered by the very people they were trying to help. Dan was 22 years old. Amy was 18.

In their growing-up days together Amy and Dan had been unusually close, and when he died she felt that a part of her 'had been amputated', that 'the light of her life had gone out' (Eldon and Eldon, 1998). Two years after Dan's death Amy had managed to channel her energies enough to enrol in college when a new and totally unexpected crisis hit. She called her mother: 'I can't remember everything about him! I'm forgetting so much. I'm scared I won't remember anything one day!' At 19, Amy entered what she describes as 'a very dark period'. All those 'what-ifferies' and 'whys'.

Just when the bereavement experts might suggest that she should be recovering from losing her darling brother, the hardest time of all hit Amy, full force. The very idea of forgetting Dan, even for an hour at a time, felt to Amy like betrayal. Bereaved parents can experience similar shock. At the point when we think we are beginning to accept our loss, new and monumentally powerful feelings emerge. For Amy, memories were beginning to blur; idiosyncrasies and normal sibling bones of contention, Dan's unique wit and sense of mischief, were all getting fuzzy in her memory. Amy takes up the story:

At first, after Dan died, I wanted to hang on to everything that he had ever owned or touched. One day I found a dusty old backpack in Dan's room. Rummaging through it, I discovered an ancient toothbrush buried under a pile of photographs and papers. I wanted to treasure it for ever ... For a long time I pulled out memories, one at a time, and used them to crawl back into the past. It gave me comfort to recall details of our lives together and helped me feel less lonely. But one horrible day, I realized my memories were fading.

At that point Amy's mother Kathy suggested that Amy make an 'angel catcher' for Dan. An angel catcher, she explained, is a version of a dream catcher. Dream catchers are popular in craft shops, circles with web threading like spiders' webs and festooned with feathers. They are intended as hangings in bedrooms and are said to 'capture' destructive dreams. Amy's angel catcher would be filled with memories of Dan. She would construct it with pictures, stories, letters, whatever reminded her of her brother. It could become a permanent keepsake to show her friends now, and some day her own children when they'd ask about their Uncle Dan. Amy put together her angel catcher for Dan. She and Kathy showed it to friends who had suffered the loss of someone dear to them. Eventually the idea became a book designed to help others catch and record the unique essence of a loved one who has died. In *Angel Catcher: A Journal of Loss and Remembrance* (Eldon and Eldon, 1998), Amy writes:

> ... as you fill the pages of this book in memory of your loved one, think about your own life. Do you have any regrets? Are you being true to yourself? Are you leading the life of your choice? Reflect on those people you love, who will one day perhaps create a journal for you. Are you letting them know how you feel? Most of all, are you creating the kind of memories you wish to leave behind? If not, now's the time to begin.

We remain in touch. Amy now hosts a public broadcasting series called Global Tribe, dedicated to the sort of tasks Dan would be proud to be part of – exploring global issues, working to save the environment, healing racism, and improving the lives of the poorest people on the planet. 'Be the Change we wish to see', in Gandhi's words. Be the difference you hope to make. However ambitious this sounds, it is without doubt that Amy (and her family) have found inspiring ways to honour Dan's memory, carry on with projects instead of being destroyed by his death, and indeed to make, and be, the difference.

Guilt

They say that being a Catholic doesn't mean you have to feel guilty, but it helps. Not that much. Lots of people who have nothing to do with Catholicism are extremely good at guilt; guilt is both the pariah and the obsession of Western culture. On the one hand, there is a continuing social trend towards not holding us responsible for our behaviour, and subsequently labelling every form of ill conduct as a disease, then prescribing a drug to knock it on the head – an undoubted cause for great rejoicing among the pharmaceutical barons. A case of this phenomenon, which crops up as a problem with bereaved children, is ADHD, or Attention Deficit Hyperactivity Disorder. I am not trying to belittle the condition of severe aggression or agitation in any child, but it is correct to point out that many children who are distracted and fidgety and disruptive are perfectly normal young humans who need extra attention, less harassed teachers in smaller classes, and love, even if it's tough love – what they don't necessarily need is to be drugged with an amphetamine.

Then there is the blame culture from which neither monarch nor menial is exempt – a good example is the burglar running away from the scene of her/his crime and who then sues the victims because the criminal was injured while trying to make a getaway. We are told that whatever happens to us is because we chose to go the way we did. So we may feel rather caught between the old devil and the deep blue sea on this one.

Being an international family, after Caitlin's death we received many hundreds of loving letters from round the world. I didn't count, but can confirm that many began with, 'Don't feel guilty because you are not guilty.' 'Don't blame yourself.' One dear friend simply wrote: 'NOT YOUR FAULT.' But, and it is a big 'but', how could she know that it wasn't my fault?

Truly, guilt has negative qualities that can take a variety of destructive forms. In the first days before we knew any details of the trail leading to Caitlin's death (it took more than two years to identify and then follow the trail which did eventually lead to accurate answers), I most certainly felt that I should have been able to prevent it; my dreams underlined these feelings. One example: Caitlin had urged for a long time that I get a mobile phone, especially since beginning an editing job in London, and I was quite a inverse snob about *not* getting one. But not long after she died I dreamt that I did have a mobile phone and rang her from the train. In the dream this phone call saved her life.

Caitlin would want no guilt, but neither would she expect any of us to arrive at a verdict of 'not guilty' until a period of self-examination had taken place. In general, a healthy guilt fosters forgiveness.

Forgiveness

Children of all ages need to understand that their actions could not have killed their brother or sister; while we regret harsh words or things left unresolved, we don't need to feel destroyed by them. Self-forgiveness is powerful. Try saying 'sorry' by writing a letter, drawing a picture, getting the feelings out. Tie it to a balloon, literal or symbolic, and let it fly away.

Reflection on sibling bereavement

Regardless of negative experiences at the time of bereavement, some extremely valuable insights have come through talking many years later about the loss of a sister or brother (Farrant, 1998).

It is impossible to make judgements about who suffers most when any one person dies. Yet it is reasonable to suppose that the grief of parents for a dead child is very different from the grief of brothers and sisters for a dead sibling and that the parents will take longer to 'process' their loss.

One sibling, now an adult, reflected that children are sometimes able to go through the grieving cycle faster than their parents, which is fine. But then a problem can arise that the child has come to a resolution and turning point, is ready to get on with the rest of life, but has a parent who is still very deeply grieving. So what to do? Try to make sure that the parent(s) get whatever help is going, and perhaps be extra patient? In which case, his or her needs still aren't being met. You are alive and wanting your parents to take an interest in what you are doing here and now. Perhaps parents might want to grieve openly at first, and then later on it may be that the parent has to have a private weep, because the living sibling has actually 'moved on' in their grief, in which case it's not a good idea for the parent to lumber them with their remaining and continuing grief.

Does belief in an afterlife make a difference? It's back to that question of what we think about death, so whatever your own belief system, the answer is 'yes'. Faith or no faith, the ongoing attachment can help transform the pain of grief into a resilient growing survival. Death ends a life; it doesn't end a relationship. The relationship struggles towards some sort of resolution that it may never find. The tasks of living are onerous, and finding a way of channelling the love for the dead child to the ongoing of life cannot be a bad thing.

I'm not talking about living in the past – rather, recognizing how bonds forged in the past can inform both our present and our future. It is never too late for siblings and parents to help one another with the burdens of grief. We mourn our dead child for the rest of our lives and the same is true for our surviving children. What is not helpful is silence. We need to be kind to ourselves, to recognize that we did the best we could at the time, and above all to keep open all channels of communication between us and our children, even if it is many years since our child died. The old chestnut that love means 'never needing to say sorry' is not useful or true. It is never too late to say, 'Sorry, I just didn't understand at the time,' for past happenings. Healing from a near-mortal wound is a lifelong process; we bear scars for ever, but it is also true that we have survived. A Pyrrhic victory maybe, but here we stand.

5

Sudden Death: Murder, Accidents and Troubled Children

I watched from the living room window as the two young police officers walked towards my front door. When they removed their hats I knew Stephen was dead. (A father)

I am mother of the murdered, the betrayed, the stolen child lured from home and tortured for why! Thrown like chaff into the windy barren field. Earth, weigh lightly on these your children, for they were no weight to you. (L. H.)

The most dangerous animal in a zoo is man.
(*Life of Pi* by Yann Martel)

Human beings have an infinite capacity for love and kindness, but mixed in with all the good is – let's not mince words – evil or, more accurately, the fruits of evil. Hatred, war, greed, suffering and murder are the underbelly of the human condition. I've occasionally glanced at my largely benevolent and likeable neighbours in our rural community and wondered if ever an Auschwitz could be built nearby, if ever an employee in any of the local shops would take employment in a concentration camp dedicated to the obliteration of a minority group branded as pariahs. Reluctantly, I think yes, it could happen. More alarmingly, let's open the door to my home, my politically correct non-violent, conflict-resolution home. Do I hate? Yes. Am I selfish? Yes. Are there people I envy? Yes. Are there people I've not forgiven? Yes. OK, I'm working hard on all these things, but without going all mystical, I assert that the negative things I do in my private space are the very activities that start wars in the wider world. Wrong is not only 'over there' – it is also looking back at me in the mirror when I floss my teeth every morning.

This book is being written at a time when revenge is in the air. International terrorism spreads a template of fear. Sabres rattle in corridors of power and our baby twenty-first century is in crisis. Our leaders call for the elimination of terrorists who threaten everyone's safety, knowing that difficult decisions in the corridors of power will bring certain death and suffering to countless innocent people. Bereaved parents mourn their own dead children and fear greatly also for the living within our own communities and our global village neighbours.

Murderers defy comprehension. What cocktail of madness leads someone to kill? Statistics speak only the numbers, not motives:

- The risk of dying as a result of homicide is highest in babies and lowest in children aged 5–14.
- Males are at greater risk of being killed than females at all ages.
- Death rates from homicides have fallen in the elderly over the past 20 years.
- In younger men, homicides have risen by about 50 per cent on average.

Stabbings and shootings have both increased, but in England and Wales shootings still account for only 10 per cent of recorded homicides (Office of National Statistics, 2003). In the United States, with its particular take on its citizens' right to bear arms, the figure is exponentially greater.

Some deaths tip the scales into a virtual murder of hope and trust in being human. The unthinkable happening, the not-do-able done. If child killings are the worst killings, then a child killing a child brings horror beyond any brink. The nature of news coverage in contemporary life means that every grisly detail of every unthinkable act is there for the reading. Parental and community forgiveness are pushed beyond endurance and imagination.

It may be possible to learn from someone whose story has taken on an international profile and who has survived an attempt on his life. On 20 April 1999, Mark Taylor, a student at Columbine High School in Littleton, Colorado, was sitting on the school lawn eating his lunch when another student called Eric Harris came up and started shooting him. Eric shot Mark maybe a dozen times in the leg, arm, chest and abdomen; no one knew the exact number of bullets because there were so many bullet tracks. Most of the bullets went 'right through me', Mark said later as he told me of the horror of that day.

Mark spent nearly two months in hospital and when I met him and his mother in October 2002, he had endured three years of follow-up operations (he will also need more operations in the future) for the wounds he received during the murderous rampage of Eric Harris, accompanied by Dylan Klebold, which killed 12 students and a teacher and ended in Eric's and Dylan's suicides.

Survivors of attempts on their lives are likely to be thorough in efforts to seek justice, and Mark Taylor is taking the pharmaceutical company Solvay to court. Solvay manufactures a medication that is called Luvox in the United States and called Faverin in the United Kingdom. Luvox/Faverin is in a class of antidepressants called selective serotonin reuptake inhibitors that interact with the 'feel-good' system in the brain, as do Prozac, Seroxat, Lustral, Efexor and Cipramil. Illegal or so-called recreational drugs that interact with the serotonergic system include LSD and Ecstasy. Mark claims that it was the brain-altering medication taken by both Eric and Dylan that caused their murderous spree. He also says, with considerable compassion, 'Eric was forced on to these drugs and I feel sorry for him ... I don't think you can hold him accountable, because he didn't know what he was doing.' Mark has been able to forgive his attacker, but still seeks justice.

Who killed my child?

The key question for most parents is, 'Who did this, who killed my child?' It is a dreadful truth that many murders are committed by a close family member or a person already known to the victim. If the person is *not* known to the family, then there is the added question, 'Why did he choose *my* child?' At first the family may not know who the murderer is, and people will react to this uncertainty in different ways. Some are consumed by a desire to know, hoping to assuage their rage and grief by having a person to blame when someone is caught. Other members of the family may feel they do not wish to know and concentrate instead on grieving for the one who has died without embarking on the quest to find out who the murderer is.

The police investigation will take its course and is not within our control. When the police have sufficient evidence, they will arrest someone; that person will then be brought to trial and be found guilty or not guilty. Reactions to the murderer can divide an already vulnerable family; it can be agonizing to see loved ones consumed with hatred and the desire for vengeance, if these are feelings we do not share. Equally, the absence of visible anger may be deeply perplexing to those who are raging about the person who has committed this terrible act.

Thinking about the murder can also bring feelings of guilt into sharp focus; you may feel that if only your child had not gone to the park, to see that friend, gone out that evening, they would still be alive. The desire to 're-run the tape' can be overpowering. There can be an instinctive but very real feeling that you have failed to protect your child. These feelings need to be shared with someone who is able to listen to them in an accepting way, rather than someone who will try to disprove them. This can be an area where counselling will be helpful. Those closest to you may find your guilt feelings not only misplaced, but unbearably painful, and so a little distance and neutrality can help.

Timo

Linda Baxter (Baxter, 2001) is a remarkable and courageous woman with whom I corresponded in my early days of editing the quarterly journal of The Compassionate Friends. After a night out with a friend, Linda's 24-year-old son Timo was murdered by six young people in a motiveless and spontaneous act of malice. The accused were found guilty of Timo's murder by a unanimous verdict. Because Timo had six attackers, his body theoretically could have been subjected to as many as six postmortems. Linda takes up the story:

> You identify your son's body. Timo's body. It is behind a glass screen. You may not touch. He is covered by a purple drape. Somehow that offends you – you thought you would see him in his clothes, as he was found. You have a caring Police Liaison Officer; she arranges it. You are numb. You think, when you get him home, you can dress him in clean jeans, T-shirt and sweatshirt, and two trainers. You shake hands with the morgue attendant, say thank you.
>
> You understand about the portmortem, you are all in favour. Three persons have been caught so far, justice must be done. You see Timo for a third time. His body is covered by a plain white sheet, as you had asked. He is still behind the glass screen. When you get him home, you will be able to look, touch, kiss him. Three more persons have to be caught. This takes four weeks.

You understand that the six defendants have the right to their own separate postmortems. You feel queasy about Timo's body being tampered with again. But justice must be done. Two further postmortems are carried out.

You are still waiting for Timo's body, to have him home and bury him in the wicker basket at the end of the far field, near the cliff top. You have to wait nine weeks altogether. The funeral director tells you that you will not recognize him. He is skin-slipped, black. Sam [Linda's husband] goes to the funeral parlour, dares to look. He comes home, tells you Timo is a mummy.

You are cheated. You have Timo home, ready for the burial ceremony. He is in the wicker coffin, flowers all round it, in the quiet room with the curtains closed. The funeral director has put Timo's clothes in the coffin as you requested; he gives you a small lock of hair. You cannot look, or touch, or kiss your son. You have to open the French windows.

A year later, Linda wrote: 'In January 2002 we planted a woodland in Timo's field – 1,500 young trees, each 50 centimetres tall, and in time for his twenty-seventh birthday. Her poem below is a response to that:

For Our Spiritual Warrior

Good planting weather.
A field of twigs – wands –
each with a cane and opaque rabbit guard –
dwarf evergreens and
mini Christmas trees,
heeled into the soil. It took four days.

Betula, Ulmas, Quercus, Populus
tremula, Sorbus, Pinus, Corylus,
Ilex, Malus, Fraxinus excelsior!

He has a holly spear, a poplar shield,
a rowan spray to ward off devilry;
ash for shelter from the gales. He can turn,
sculpt, build cradles and boats, smell the sweetest
pine, talk to the aspen, whisper to the
winds; glide through oak's threshold to the light.

Be not afraid:
one and a half thousand rune-staffs
safeguard you on your way.

Linda Baxter has taken up creative writing and written a book of poetry. Taken a degree. Timo would have been hugely proud.

Ruairidh

Pat Neil is another friend who came into my life as a mysterious mercy, the kind that follows tragedy and pours balm on the unbearable. Pat served for eight years as editor of The Compassionate Friends' then quarterly newsletter. Here she reflects on her son Ruairidh's death:

> The sound of an ambulance siren, that's all it takes to start the memories ... Yet, at the time, and contrary to all my preconceived ideas about maternal extra-sensory perception, I suffered no shiver of premonition or foreboding. As the local doctor on call, my husband was already on his way to the accident site. The next time I saw him, after I'd been to pick up our younger son from school, he was standing stock still at our back door. 'It's Ruairidh, he's gone, he's dead.' Not recognizing the crashed car, he had discovered his son, unable to save his life but in time to hold him as he took his last breath.
>
> That was where we started from, April in 1987. Ruairidh was our elder son, aged 12, when he was given the lift that ended in disaster for two families. Since then we have driven that road countless times, and re-created in our minds his last journey. We have two other children, who have their own stories to tell.
>
> What about this word *accident*? A 'road traffic incident' is the way it is described these days. But for me, trying to get to grips with what had happened, catastrophe exploding into the humdrum day, the concept of *accident* was of crucial significance. It was my first intellectual struggle in the fog of shock and emotional despair. What *is* an accident? Given that the young driver of the car had supposedly taken a corner too fast, there were still a whole string of tiny coincidences which meant that other more reliable drivers were not in charge of the car, that our son had been sitting in the seat which took the brunt of the smash, that another friend had missed the trip altogether. If any one of these

had been different our child might have been alive today. So it was the first lesson in acceptance, of the irrelevance of guilt or blame for the small decisions which we take, or which are taken for us, every day, and which do not, in the normal course of things, end in tragedy.

'How do you cope?' was the most frequent question in the early months. The answer that was right for then is equally right for now: 'I wake up in the morning. And I have to do the day.' The inevitability of the day dawning, and time having to be filled as best I could, was in those days merely a desperate handle to hang on to. Five minutes, ten minutes, I could do that. But now, 15 years on, the day still dawns, and it is still up to me how I spend it, although I do have a longer perspective to play with these days. So many things changed that springtime, the watershed between life as we knew it and life as it now had to be lived. And the way I live now has everything to do with that April morning when I lost one of my children. The appreciation of what I still have came only slowly, but is now the keystone of my belief structure. The small things mean proportionately more, immensely more. The first restoration of pleasure was picking up a warm egg from the nest; an unexpected gift from one of my hens helped me to understand that it was going to be natural events, rooted in life and growth, which would help to build the stairway up out of the pit. And I knew I would have to use all my powers to do this, ones I was familiar with and others I had yet to discover.

I do not have a religious faith, have never had one, although I was educated in the Church of England and know and love the old language of the King James Bible. I have never believed in a life after death, and do not yearn for it. Although I sometimes still ache and rage for Ruairidh's lost chances, I am now mostly acquiescent to our lot, that his time was so short upon the earth. He was here, he brought joy, we loved him and he is gone. I weep for what he might have had, what I see our other children experiencing as adults. But for my own tranquillity I need the conceptual simplicity of a life lived, a life ended; endless searching is to me an affront to acceptance, to the hard realities of life. And of death.

I know that to many this is a desperately negative, bleak and unconsoling sort of credo. But I know too that I'm a positive person, and to me it is an honest and joyful celebration of life: that we are born, we grow, some of us live to set seed, some of us are cut down in flower. And tomorrow another round of growth will begin. There is here a completeness which I find totally spiritual, totally at one with everything. The key for me was reading the words of bereaved mothers and fathers from different continents and cultures and in different periods of history. How similar was our pain, even if we might not have understood each other face to face. But the powerful ropes of loss, of grief for our sons and daughters, joined us inseparably down the ages. It made such sense.

The writer Rumer Godden wrote about the house with four rooms: an Indian proverb offers this analogy, that we ourselves are the house, containing a physical, a mental, an emotional and a spiritual room. We need to go into each room every day, even if it is only to keep it aired, or we are not a complete person. When my son died I lived mostly in the emotional room, sometimes dashing aimlessly in and out of the others, but as time passed I found I could – indeed, needed to – visit the others on a regular basis, with a purpose.

I now live relatively comfortably in all my four rooms; a balance has been achieved. Perhaps Ruairidh wouldn't see much of a change in me if he reappeared tomorrow, but I know that I'm a different person, and I live differently, not only because he died, but because he lived.

Even the most pious among us knows we can't always expect comfort from faith. Pat's comment on belief reminds me of a professor who quipped that atheism was the natural outcome of a happy childhood; a believer himself, Professor Maiden added that God loves atheists best of all. I repeated this to my brother Roy, a fierce atheist, during a heated discussion where he plucked out the Richard Dawkins chestnut about religion being a malignant virus. 'Don't tell me that someone who doesn't exist loves me best of all!' We fell about laughing. He knows that he can't prove God's non-existence any more than I can prove otherwise, beyond saying that absence of proof isn't proof of absence.

One woman, whose 25-year-old son and his pregnant wife were both murdered, wrote:

The first things we coped with were the shock, pain, numbness, bitterness. Possibly fortunately for us [she and her husband] we uplifted one another, and when one was down and upset the other gained strength. The hardest part is acceptance; it may sound strange, but I tried turning thoughts the other way round, thinking how proud I was to have been Kevin's mum – how would I have felt being the murderer's mum? (The murderer in this case gave himself up and was sentenced to life.)

Comfort can come in small vehicles, and in this case with wheels. Dr Lindsay Neil, Pat's husband, wrote of the comfort of driving his car (Neil, 1999):

After my son was killed my car was my haven. I could weep there in privacy; there was no phone, I didn't have to meet and talk to anyone and I knew roughly how long I had on my own. The trouble is that tears obscure your vision and can make driving a hazard. Laybys are useful; you can regain control before getting back amongst the traffic. Thoughts can also stray far from the road situation in front of you, and I'm sure many of you are familiar with the phenomenon of suddenly realizing that you can't remember the details of the last few miles of your journey. We need to be aware that grief can make us less than perfect drivers. There is an uncomfortable irony in this if our own child has been killed in a road traffic accident [as was Lindsay's son Ruairidh]. But times to weep are vital. Men sometimes find it difficult to shed tears in front of other people, although Churchill did, Wellington did, and my grandfather, a Church of Scotland minister, did after the death from leukaemia of his young son. Nevertheless, I blessed my car as a cocoon to weep in.

Murder and sudden death: a scenario

The following is an amalgam of many parents' experiences of the events following the loss of a child to murder or other sudden death, told from the parents' perspective.

The news sounds as if it were from another planet. In an instant, our whole family's existence, the totality of life itself, is changed for ever, as the words are spoken. Sometimes the shock is a cushion from reality for a while; we seem to be watching the tragedy unfold through dimmed spectacles, this dreadful news is not about us, not about our family. But it is.

For parents who are told our child has been murdered or found dead, there is so much to confront, for murder and sudden death are:

- Always unexpected – there is no preparation for this moment.
- Often violent – someone/something has destroyed the life of our child.
- Often deliberate – in the case of murder, someone has intentionally committed this deed.

Bringing the news

The police will most likely be the bearers of this terrible news, and they arrive unannounced at our door. There is no easy way to give or receive such news, but the manner in which it is brought is important.

What we need is clear information, stated in a compassionate way and in everyday language. When we are in shock, we may not take in what is being said. Some of us ask our messenger to repeat things. We want to ask questions, and the police may or may not have answers. We ask the police to leave contact details in writing. In our case, we were assigned a 'family liaison officer', to keep us informed.

The police don't have all the information we need; they couldn't tell us how, or even when, our child died, whether death was quick, whether he/she knew what was happening, whether he/she suffered. At this early stage, the police focus on arresting a possible offender, who in some cases might be one of the family.

Missing children

A different set of circumstances arises with some of us: our child is missing but no body has been found. We still hope that our child is alive and well. This hope may be abruptly shattered by the discovery of a body, or it may fade over time – and their body may never be found. Both uncertainty and knowledge are terrible in their different ways. Many of us feel that never finding our child's body is the worst possible thing.

Immediate practicalities

There is a desperate need to tell the family, but we are in such a state of shock that we can't think clearly. The police step in here, and suggest that we ask maybe a close friend to help to begin the necessary telephone calls and communications. Murder and sudden death bring added urgency. There are two pressing needs: our need to tell family and close friends before they hear it through the media, and the need for the police to begin their investigations as quickly as possible.

If defined as murder, the death becomes public property and we have no control over what information is released. It can be very difficult to reach all those extended family members and close friends we wish to tell before the news is made public. The presence of the media, whether we feel this to be intrusive or helpful, is an added burden.

There is a further complication if we are dealing with a murder and it was committed in the family home. The police investigation will then demand that our home is sealed to protect the evidence, and there can be no access. Thus, at a most crucial time, we are deprived of our familiar base – and may also be separated from vital possessions, such as clothes, money, address books, photographs, etc. Later, there can also be emotional and practical problems in reopening and retaking possession of the place in which our child has died or been killed.

The postmortem

Immediately after the death, the police will report to the coroner, or procurator fiscal in Scotland, who will arrange for our child's body to be taken to the mortuary and for a pathologist to carry out a postmortem to find out the cause of death. We have the right to ask for an independent postmortem or for a copy of the pathologist's report; we can ask for it to be sent to our GP so that she or he can go through it with us and explain the details. We will need to ask about the possible cost of both of these. An added painful complication in death through murder is that each defendant has the right to ask for a separate postmortem and this can delay the release of the body for the funeral.

When a murder happens abroad

Circumstances are even more complicated if our son or daughter dies in another country. We are often made to feel powerless and out of control. We find that, without preparation or back-up, we must cope with that country's legal system, language and communication.

Some countries must complete burial or cremation with great swiftness, so that even while in the first numb stages of shock, we are required to act very quickly in order to bring our child's body home, quite possibly for an independent postmortem. The cost of travel, of translating documents and of obtaining local legal advice can be prohibitive, and some of us are unable to do all that we would wish. When there is a later trial abroad, misunderstandings can easily arise; it can be very hard to follow the proceedings and to understand what is happening and why. In some countries, Victim Support (United Kingdom) can help with information (see Helpful Contacts at the end of the book), as well as the Foreign Office and the British Embassy in the country where our child died.

Surviving children

When murder or sudden death happens, normality ceases. It is not possible to protect surviving children from this; they *will* be affected (see Chapter 4). We tell younger children enough to satisfy their questions at the time, to reassure them of our love for them, to tell them that we understand their feelings of fear, and that the police are trying hard to catch the person responsible or solve the mystery surrounding their sibling's death. While we won't burden them with terrible details, we know it is better that they hear the facts from us rather than in the playground. We will be honest – and try not to have secrets or pretend, even to our very young children who know when the adults they love are distraught. We try to be open about our feelings. It is hard enough to be a child at such a time, without the added worry of thinking, 'What are they *not* telling me?' We do lots of hugging and crying, being physically close, and this helps us and our children to be able to grieve and to feel that loved ones are united in that grief.

We are most aware of not being able to help older children, who so often feel helpless, hopeless and alienated. Just when we most need one another, and need to help one another, we can feel pushed apart (see Chapter 4).

Our child's body

An essential part of parenting is the physical care of our child's body and its needs; even when our daughter or son is an adult, the memory of such care is a powerful force. Murder and suspicious death make it impossible to continue that care; the child's body becomes the property of the state rather than that of the family. Many of us suffer intense pain and anger at being prevented from caring and making proper arrangements for our child's body (see Timo's story, page 101).

It is essential that someone identifies the body; and this is a difficult and painful hurdle to overcome, especially where there has been visible injury. Yet, if the injuries are carefully explained, the reality can be less distressing than the imaginings. Our child's body will usually be seen at the mortuary and arrangements will vary. We do have the right to see our child, although some of us are not able to touch her/him. Many of us wish to see our child more than once and most mortuaries are understanding of this need, especially if there is likely to be a long delay in releasing the body into the care of a funeral director. Some of us ask for a lock of our child's hair. We look to others to be as sensitive as possible to all the circumstances.

The police

Police training does not always prepare officers adequately for the emotional issues that arise from a suspicious death, and we may need to seek help from other agencies, both professional and support groups, such as SAMM (Support After Murder and Manslaughter) (see Helpful Contacts at the end of the book).

Victim Support

This service offers trained volunteers experienced in helping our families through the aftermath of suspicious deaths and murder. These volunteers may help with the practical issues and offer to accompany us on some essential visits. They can also act as intermediaries with the police, coroner (procurator fiscal in Scotland), mortuary officials and other agencies, if we wish them to do so. Such trained help, when available, may continue through the later events, including support at the trial. The Crown Court Witness Service can also be of great help.

The press and other media

The media will usually be interested in a murder. They see it as a gripping human interest story and will want to exploit it to the full. The police press officer may be able to help and advise regarding contacts with the media, as may the Victim Support volunteer. Our experience as families bereaved in this way suggests that it is a good idea to give the media a brief statement, together with a photograph of our child, to avoid inaccuracies. We have now 'done our bit' and will wish for privacy. It is often helpful to ask a friend to answer the phone at this time, to screen incoming calls. Many of us will want to brace ourselves for the fact that the media, as well as the public, have the right to attend both the inquest and the trial.

The inquest (not applicable in Scotland)

The coroner will open the inquest as soon as possible after the postmortem. The inquest is an inquiry, conducted by a coroner, to establish the facts of the identity of the dead person and when, where and how the death occurred. The inquest is not concerned with who caused the death, because that will be investigated at the trial.

It will be necessary for someone to have identified our child's body and for that person to make a statement on oath; this statement can be presented in writing at the inquest. Once the cause of death and the current state of the police investigation are reported, the inquest will be adjourned, while the criminal investigation continues. It will not be formally closed until after the trial. If no one is charged with a murder, an inquest hearing will take place.

Throughout these procedures we need to be kept informed. Many of us exercise the right to instruct a solicitor both to ask questions on our behalf and to request that particular witnesses are called. It is the coroner who conducts these hearings and decides who should give evidence. Legal aid does not cover these expenses.

After the initial inquest has established the cause of death, an interim death certificate can be given, although a formal death certificate will not be issued until the inquest is completed after the trial. Our child's body will be released by the coroner only when she or he is satisfied that the defence has had the opportunity to ask for a postmortem. This can lead to a very long delay, if the police inquiry is lengthy, or if no one is charged. It causes great distress to us and to our friends when the funeral is delayed for weeks, or even months. During this time, the body is the responsibility of the coroner. Only when the coroner gives permission can we or our funeral director remove our child's body to a chapel of rest. Even if the case never comes to court, our child's body will ultimately be released for the funeral, although the police investigation will never be officially closed. The Compassionate Friends has leaflets on many relevant matters, including the titles *On Inquests*, *Preparing Your Child's Funeral* and *The Death of a Child and the Legal System* (see Helpful Contacts at the end of the book).

The funeral

The long delay and the feeling that all living is suspended, and that the grieving is impeded, disappear when the body of our son or daughter is released for burial. There will have been time to reflect and plan for the funeral, to make it the tribute and farewell that we need and that our child deserves.

. It is important to take control of the public aspects of the funeral. We may want a small private ceremony, or an occasion when the local community can join family and friends in saying farewell. The media should respect our choice, but it's a good idea to make that choice known, so that an important and long-awaited day is not marred by unwanted intrusions.

The time after the funeral is often one of loneliness and isolation; the funeral has been the focus of attention, and there may now seem to be a withdrawal of interest and concern. There are some practical matters to attend to, but the central issue remains unresolved. Contact with the police may be infrequent at this time if they have nothing to report; indeed, we may almost be made to feel that our legitimate enquiries are a nuisance ('Don't call us, we'll call you'). Some of us ask our Victim Support volunteer to liaise with the police on our behalf, and we may well also ask to meet together on a regular basis.

All of us, without exception, feel very vulnerable at this time. This may be made worse if we hear rumours about suspects, evidence, or even about our child's lifestyle. When a suspect is arrested the police should inform us directly, and continue to give updates on court hearings, changes of plea, applications for bail, etc. Our Victim Support volunteer will have experience of the court procedures, which is invaluable.

The trial (cases of murder and manslaughter)

Careful preparations can do something to mitigate the ordeal. If possible, we will want to see the courtroom before the trial begins, and to know whether some seating is set aside for the family (not least so that we are not forced to sit beside the relatives of the accused). Hopefully we will have been told if new information is to be disclosed or if the defendant has changed his or her plea.

The pathologist's report on the postmortem will include detailed descriptions of the injuries to our child, for which we try to prepare ourselves. Scene-of-death photographs or other items of evidence may be passed to the jury. We know it's coming, and can – so far as this is possible – be braced for the reality.

Once the legal proceedings begin, the role of the police can be a shock. During the investigation, the police have been in charge, and in Scotland we will have also been in touch with the procurator fiscal. Once the case comes to court, however, it is the judge and the lawyers, representing the legal system, who are in control. The lawyers are there to prosecute or to defend; this can lead to manipulation and distortion, with no possibility of comeback from us, the dead child's family. We often feel we are representing our child in court, and try to be strong for them; but, unless we are called as witnesses, we have no voice. We may be distressed by how little our child is spoken of as a person during the trial, by how technical and 'wooden' the proceedings are, and by the intrusive presence of the media in court.

Here again Victim Support and Witness Support volunteers can act as guides and help with a press statement at the end of the trial. When the accused enters a guilty plea, the proceedings can be very brief. We may find this shocking; little may have been said about the actual murder, and damaging comments about our child may go unchallenged.

The verdict and the sentence may be yet another great shock to many of us. A 'not guilty' (or in Scotland 'not proven') verdict leaves the whole question unresolved: is the jury mistaken, or did someone else kill our child? Even a 'guilty' verdict may generate feelings that the sentence is inadequate, that the murderer will be free to carry on with normal life before he or she has been properly punished. For others, however, there will be feelings of intense relief that the judgement has been made. If the defendant is convicted of murder, the sentence will automatically be 'life', or sometimes 'life with a recommendation that you serve X years'. The judge then makes a recommendation to the Home Secretary. We parents may not be informed officially of the 'tariff' or time to be spent in prison, although it should be possible to find out.

The attention of the media will immediately focus on our reaction to the verdict and sentence; again, preparation can help, such as a prepared statement, read by a lawyer or other chosen person.

The aftermath

We must now learn to live with the outcome of the trial, the length of sentence, parole, remission, the possible continued presence of the murderer's family within our community, and how we will feel when our child's killer is released, perhaps to return to his or her nearby home. In the short term, many of us suffer great emotional stress immediately after the ending of the court case, and have much need of supportive friends. Emotions may have been suppressed during the trial and these can now resurface in an overwhelming torrent of pent-up grief and rage.

The police are now free at last to return our child's possessions; they will have been held as evidence until this time. Sometimes this is handled insensitively and further distress caused. It is very painful suddenly to hold those things that our child had with them when they died. It can help to have a friend or Victim Support volunteer with us, and for the handing over to be done gently, in a private space, with some recognition of these intimate and primal feelings.

With their work complete, the police inevitably move on to other cases and this too can leave us feeling isolated, ignored and rejected. In the long term, we must find our own way of adapting to what has happened, a way of living with what cannot be changed, and of working through the pain and grief so that life can somehow continue, now that nothing will ever be the same for us.

Feelings

The savage circumstances surrounding murder will inevitably create unbearable waves of emotion. As the shock and numbness wear off, we wonder how it is possible to survive such extremes of anger, rage, depression, guilt and sorrow. We are aware that it is important to be able to express these emotions in one way or another. Some of us need to talk and weep, exhausting family, friends and maybe counsellors, as we give words to our sorrow and devastation. Others of us may suffer from frightening physical symptoms such as palpitations, nausea, insomnia and very specific physical pain; we may need our doctor to give us reassurance that these are all symptoms of grief.

Panic attacks are common for us, the families of murder victims and violent crime, stemming from the understandable feeling that the world is suddenly a crazy, hostile place where unthinkable things occur without warning or reason. Depression is also normal (see Chapter 2), and it is natural to feel hostility, anger and hatred towards the person who killed our child, though not everyone does so. These feelings may focus on the suspect, if one is arrested, but can also be directed at the police, the law, other family members, or even against ourselves.

If no one is caught, some of us try to release the emotional vacuum through fantasy, especially the fantasy of revenge. If these intense negative emotions are not confronted, they can become buried in a way that will be damaging and may lead to later problems. Professional help, or the support of others who have been through a similar tragedy, can help us through these terrible feelings.

Many people bereaved by murder experience great difficulties when they try to resume normal activities. Life seems meaningless and empty, things that before brought pleasure are now without attraction, and even laughter may bring a feeling of guilt. It can be very hard for friends to see such changes persisting for years after the murder; they may well wonder if we will ever live normally again. But it is not possible to hasten the process of reintegration into a world that so cruelly destroyed our child; we can only make the journey at our own pace.

Unresolved murders

Some of us have to find a way of adapting to long-term uncertainty, perhaps never knowing what happened to our son or daughter, who killed them, or even whether he or she is alive or dead. For the police, an unsolved murder file is never closed, but we need to find a way of grieving that will make it possible to continue with the rest of our lives, and this is a very tall order. Such anguish cannot be fully understood by those who have not experienced it. Decisions will need to be made about the possibility of holding a memorial service, even though no body has been found. For some of us this feels like the abandonment of hope, but for others it is the right decision. Experience shows that those of us who do arrange a celebration of our beloved child's life, even though we don't know whether they are still alive, will not regret having done so.

The death of a difficult or troubled child

A purportedly reliable rule of thumb is that six to eight people are directly and permanently affected by a sudden death. In my experience, this is a conservative estimate. All deaths, and most especially the violent deaths of children, have huge repercussions, not only on immediate family and friends, but often on entire communities. There may well be ruined memories that place barriers in the way of loving witnesses/survivors finding a way to pick up the threads of a meaningful life following such a death.

We live in a harsh world where too often even our friends are quick with judgement and slow with mercy. Some bereaved people have to bear not only the burden of losing their child, but also must deal with the opprobrium of a society that is critical for a variety of reasons. She or he may have died because of an addiction to drugs or alcohol or solvent abuse, perhaps while committing a crime, or might have been responsible for the death of others. He or she may have suffered from a variety of physical and/or mental disabilities which contributed to destructive behaviours and subsequently fed public misunderstanding.

Even in organizations dedicated to providing support to all loved ones through the grief of losing a child, I've observed that people who have lost difficult and troubled children are too often stigmatized. One recent if extreme incident still chills to the marrow: a bereaved father was speaking to a group of similarly bereaved people about his adult son's death as a result of heroin. The son who died happened to be a young doctor and, without hesitation, another member of the group said, 'We can't have doctors overdosing on drugs. Try to look at it this way – the fewer drug addicts in this world the better. The only good druggie is a dead druggie.' Thankfully, another member of the group then asked how many people present led drug-free lives. This calming 'let he who is without sin cast the first stone' – or, more accurately, 'let he who has never been stoned cast out the sinner' – question did the trick.

Annette Rogers was a good loving parent who did her best for her talented daughter Lauren. She believed that Lauren would never use drugs, but Lauren did, and got mixed up with a bad crowd. She turned to prostitution and heroin, and tragically died of an overdose. 'I discovered there was still enormous stigma attached to my daughter's death, along the lines "but she chose to take heroin, she was just another junkie". Perhaps this is the case, but I have still lost my beautiful, intelligent and beloved daughter.' Annette has since founded a support service for parents/families of drug misusers (see Helpful Contacts at the back of the book).

It is a natural part of grief to idealize our dead children – really good kids become saints and ordinary kids become perfect. Where, then, is the space for loved ones to speak about our difficult and troubled children? Too often in support groups for bereaved parents we hear that all our children are perfect: distinction students, Scouts, head girls, prefects, choristers, happy, honest as the day is long, charming, never a nano-second's trouble. None of the older ones, heaven forbid!, would ever have touched alcohol or experimented with drugs or behaved in ways that would make their parents cringe! Imagine yourself in this support group. Are you going to say, 'Actually, my Janey was bombed out of her brain on every drug you can think of, and then had sex with half the football team . . . And she'd handed these tabs out to her friends, none of whom had ever tried anything . . .' Or, 'Well actually, my son was gay and got bullied and trapped because he was a bit promiscuous . . .' Or, 'My daughter's boyfriend pushed her off a bridge in a jealous frenzy.'

The likelihood is that parents of troubled children may not even be at such a meeting in the first place unless someone has made it absolutely clear that the group is gathering in full knowledge that none of our children are perfect, and that it is important to be able to say so. Unhappily, and far too often, the conspiracy of silence attending their lives will follow these children after their deaths. Parents of troubled children will most likely be silenced by the intimidation of (pretended) perfection, the fear of judgement, just as too often they were silenced from talking about the child's problems when they were alive.

Parents already often feel blamed and criticized – 'Well, they would behave that way, wouldn't they, coming from that background'. Or there may be an implication that the child 'brought it on herself/himself', 'got what they deserved', and that therefore families are not entitled to the same respect or sympathy for grief that is shown to others. Certainly this can be the case in suicide (see Chapter 6).

Sometimes parents and siblings have been on a treadmill of trauma long before the final tragedy of death, running from doctor to therapist and back, to the school, to the police, the social services, always hoping to resolve a child's troubles. The level of anxiety may seem never to let up. What's he up to? Where is she? Why hasn't he come home when he said he would? It may feel sometimes as if we are taking on the whole world in fighting for the well-being of our child, rushing off to bail her out of jail, trying Tough Love, Soft Love, Big Love, Post-traumatic Parental Love, Pooped-out Love.

Our troubled child may have tried medication and other 'cure all' programmes. Sometimes parents lose touch entirely for stretches of time, and the first news for a long time is the one we wished fervently we'd never hear. With a troubled child there is a real sense in which grief has been going on for a long time already, the time when she/he seemed to go into a space beyond reach, beyond help – death can be the final phase of a seemingly endless nightmare. Even as the bleak pall of grief descends, there can be a sense of relief. The sense of walking on broken glass is gone – and parents may then feel guilty about feeling a strange but definite relief.

Most cruelly, the death may occur just when our son or daughter shows signs of recovering health and well-being, and then spins off to disaster. For friends of those bereaved in this situation, it's a matter of trying to stand in the shoes of the parents of the dead child who was a joy rider, those who deserve the same concern and kindness as those who lose a child to cancer. We may well feel shame if our child's actions have damaged others, or great rage at what the child has done to themselves and to the family, while at the same time being intensely protective. Perhaps most of all, and most impossible of all, we wish we could turn back the clock. Parents of troubled children loved them just as much as all parents adore their children, and need to be able to grieve their losses and hopefully recover the joyful memories in the totality of their lives.

Rumours will abound after the death of our troubled child; people may avoid us. We may feel ostracized, and isolation can be a big temptation, feeling that it is better not to try. First times of anything can be terrible, from returning to work to simply going out for the newspaper. Hopefully with a great deal of help and support from those who care, we will be able to say: 'Cheryl was a difficult kid; things went so wrong and out of control. She was also beautiful, bright, loving, proud and sensitive.' The contradictions of a troubled child's life make the sweet memories sweeter. All troubled children deserve to be remembered in the wholeness of their life. Growing towards this point, however, is likely to be slow, and will probably not occur until long after others have forgotten the circumstances in which they died.

HIV/AIDS

Life expectancy in Zimbabwe of babies born in 1993, 61 years. Life expectancy in Zimbabwe of babies born in 1998 due to the prevalence of HIV/AIDS, 39 years.

(*Independent on Sunday*, November 1998)

AIDS remains the world's leading infectious killer, causing six million deaths a year (Dunn, 2000). It is more common than tuberculosis, diarrhoea or lung infections and is only exceeded by strokes, heart and pulmonary disease. Most new diagnoses are in African cities.

About 20 years ago, my son's honorary godfather, affectionately called Big Foot because of his size 16 shoes, died after a protracted illness. Jim lived in California, and the last time we heard his voice was the week before he died in his parents' home. We were told that he had pneumonia. Not until after Jim's death did his best friend, my nephew Curtis, tell me the whole story. We knew Jim was gay, but so what? He was also the best adult role model imaginable for our son. Curtis told us that Jim had died from HIV/AIDS, but that Jim's parents could not face this fact, so the official cause of death was to be pneumonia. When Jim had spent time in a Christian (*sic*) hospital, he was treated like a biblical leper, and had laughed sadly when telling Curtis about the time he was walking along the corridor, stopped to take a drink from the water fountain, and was grabbed from behind by a male nurse who said, 'Uh-uh, buddy, this fountain's for human beings.'

Thankfully, times have changed as the facts of the disease have emerged. Although originally regarded as a disease of gay men, this misconception is no longer the case. The emphasis in the United Kingdom is now on heterosexual partners, and effective health education has made some difference in the incidence of HIV/AIDS in this country. More than half of the positive diagnoses are women. There is a 12–30 per cent chance that a woman can pass the HIV virus on to her unborn child, but it is difficult to be sure whether this has happened until the child is tested at 18 months.

People with more experience of HIV-related deaths are more likely to treat them like any other. However, it is not rare, especially in more provincial communities, for undertakers to insist that the body goes into a heavy-duty plastic body bag which they do not permit to be reopened. They may also label the body and body bag as well as the attendant paperwork. The Terrence Higgins Trust suggests that if a body bag is to be used, partners and friends should be aware that they may not be allowed to see the body again, and any necessary religious rites should be performed first.

Gay and lesbian parents, partners and children

Same-sex partners have as yet no legal status in England and Wales, although there is hoped-for change in the political air. In the past it was sadly common for parents to reject homosexuality in children and there are still too often cases of estrangement and unspoken 'stuff' within the family. If the child who has died was 'in the closet', there can be conflicts about how information is handled after the death. Some parents will only discover their child's lifestyle at the inquest.

A dilemma can arise if the son or daughter had a partner. If she/he suffered a terminal illness, parents will often want to be carers – thus at times excluding the partner and friends. Shedding a lifetime of prejudice in a short period is not easy, especially in times of great stress. Too often recriminations are common, just when the dying person would want parents, friends and partner to be unified, and when warmth and unity are paramount.

In cases where bereaved parents are in a same-sex partnership and the child is from a previous marriage or partnership, the same sensitivity is called for as in a step-parent or adopted-child situation. It is an unfortunate fact that the child's 'number two mum or dad', who has supported the dead child in every possible way, is sometimes made to feel invisible or unnecessary, or both. The Lesbian and Gay Bereavement Project can be helpful in such situations (see Helpful Contacts at the back of the book).

A 'tomorrow plan'

If we lose a child to murder or accidental death, or our offspring die through involvement with drugs and danger, or their lifestyles were not mainstream, we will know that no one can tell us how to survive such a life-shattering event. Each individual and each family has to tread their own path through the darkness. However, following the long weeks and months of funeral, inquest and trial, these are some ways in which parents can honour their memory (see also Chapter 7):

- Work for changes in the law. After the Columbine massacre in the United States, survivor Mark Taylor (see p. 99) campaigned for Walmart to stop selling firearms over the counter, and was featured in Michael Moore's Oscar-winning film *Bowling for Columbine*. Two other examples are the Snowdrop campaign following the Dunblane massacre, and RoadPeace, dedicated to bringing greater safety to our streets and highways, and saving lives.
- Make a place for good memories dedicated to your child: a seat in a public place, a garden, a trust or award for something your child cared about.
- Try to learn to focus on the life and joy of your child while they lived. If the roles were reversed and you had been murdered, you would not want them to be consumed with hatred so that yet another destruction was wrought. How do you think they would wish you to survive and be strong and positive?

Wherever you are, it is a lifelong struggle to find a way to integrate a child's death with the rest of life. Many will think that you have 'got over it' when they see you outwardly in control of your life and emotions, but the turmoil and anguish may still rage within. It is at times like these that befriending and self-help groups, who know the difference between the appearance and the constant inward struggle to maintain a semblance of normality, can offer support and understanding as you endeavour to rebuild your life and to make long-term sense of the savage event that has destroyed a precious member of it.

TCF (The Compassionate Friends), of which FBbH (Families Bereaved by Homicide) is part, and SAMM (Support After Murder and Manslaughter) are organizations that offer help (see Helpful Contacts at the back of the book). TCF has a range of leaflets, a national postal library, a quarterly journal and a nationwide network of bereaved parent contacts. Parents need not leave the child who has died behind in the struggle to find a way to live. It is my hope that

6

Suicide: When the World Has Gone Out

A friend is the one who comes in when the world has gone out.
(Caitlin Hurcombe's diary)

Parents who lose a child to suicide share much in common with other bereaved people, though bereavement reactions are likely to be more intense and long-lasting after suicide. There are no farewells. When suicide is violent, there is the added legacy that is shared with relatives of murder victims. The unique factor in suicide is having to live with the thought that the death of the child was a self-inflicted execution, and may have been deliberately chosen. We are devastated by the thought that our child suffered a despair so intense that it led to self-annihilation, by the inherent violence, by the implied statement that whoever is left cannot help any more.

Every year some 5,000 people kill themselves in England and Wales; and at least 200,000 people attempt suicide each year, although the true number is likely to be much higher. In the age group 15–19, nearly 800 people in 100,000 try to kill themselves – this is double the number that did so ten years ago. Young people are at the highest risk of suicide, and the clumsily labelled 'completed suicides' or 'successful suicides' are increasing more rapidly in this group than any other. Suicide is the third most important cause of death for young people, and a person who has tried to kill themselves previously is more than 1,000 times as likely to try again than someone who has not (Office of National Statistics).

Contrary to prevailing opinion, suicide is an oft-considered option – a permanent solution to a temporary problem – in our culture. We don't like to say how often it is thought about, not least because we fear that if we speak about it we may perpetuate an epidemic. Suicide rates in England and Wales vary widely according to regional authority areas (Dunn, 2000). Figures are highest in areas where factors such as unemployment, one-parent families and chronic illness are pressing problems. During the crises of BSE and the foot and mouth outbreak, suicides in farming communities rose sharply. In one large metropolitan area, Manchester, 10 per cent of men were diagnosed as 'clinically' depressed. There were 208 suicides per 100,000 population among men between the ages of 15 and 44, and the female rate was 2.3 times higher than the national average. At the other end of the scale only 4 young male suicides per 100,000 population occurred during the same period in South Herefordshire. Lower figures are typical of more prosperous areas.

Solo parents form another vulnerable group. Changing patterns of kinship have increased social isolation, and single-person households doubled in the latter half of the twentieth century. In the area of south London where my son lives, the rate of female suicide doubled the national average, and the most vulnerable group were solo mothers, often trapped in poor housing and high-rise flats.

Self-destruction once carried with it some powerful disincentives – if the prospect of hell did not put the would-be suicide off, the fear of prison might (Hill, 1995); of course, the fear of prison could also make those vulnerable to suicide more determined to 'get it right' too. None the less, suicide has undergone a rapid rehabilitation. The crime of the 1950s has become, in the euthanasia debate of the 1990s and early 2000s, an action affiliated to personal dignity. Suicide has become more acceptable.

A benign concept of death, a loosening of moral prohibitions and an emphasis on personal freedom have combined to create relatively liberal attitudes; and it seems likely that greater tolerance has reduced the number of psychological obstacles standing between young people and suicide. There is also some evidence that liberal and secular mores encourage acceptance of euthanasia and suicide as an aspect of individual rights. This is difficult to quantify, but European countries suffering the sharpest drop in church membership in the 1960s and mid-1980s suffered sharper increases in youth suicide (Hill, 1995).

The aftermath of suicide

The families of those who have died by suicide have to cope with feelings of distress that go beyond normal grief (Albery *et al.*, 1997). Suicide still carries with it a heavy social stigma, and families can become ensnared in a sometimes hopeless search to find out why a child felt so desperate. A sister recalls the loss of her brother:

> In April 1999 my brother drove to a bridge near our home and jumped off on to the road below. He had been receiving

antidepressant medication for only a week. When I heard the news I thought it was all just a bad dream. Something so awful could never happen to a wonderful person like my brother. I realized that there is no way that things could be worse.

I know this may sound horrid, but I feel envious of people grieving for a child who died of cancer or in a car accident, or even murdered. This is because they have someone or something, a disease or a perpetrator, to blame. I don't want to blame my brother! I loved him so much. I still absolutely cringe if I have to relate what happened to him. I don't want to be ashamed of him, so I tell myself it was the depression that killed him. You need someone or something to blame. My family is being torn apart by his death. We will never be the same loving family again.

Drugs and suicide

The majority of suicides appear to involve either street drugs, alcohol or medication; and the alarming increase in the suicide of our children runs in tandem with the appearance (since 1990) of medications targeted to treat a variety of conditions common to young people. It's fair to observe: a) that a proportion of those who died were taking medication to treat one or more of these conditions, and b) that an exponential increase in deaths by suicide is not supposed to be what happens when a medication works.

Telling children about a death by suicide

In an article aimed at telling children about suicide ('Talking about Suicide with Young Children') Margaret Harvey makes a generally telling point (Harvey, 2001):

> It is always hard to tell children that someone they loved has died. We are right to worry about hurting them or stretching their understanding beyond their capacity, about 'shattering the bright canopy of love and protection' with which we try to surround them. But it has to be done.
>
> There is no easy way to talk to children about any death of a loved one, and suicide comes at the top of the scale of difficulty, near impossibility. All our instincts are to protect our children

from harm; we worry rightly about finding a way to help them understand when we ourselves are floundering in a sea of 'Whys?' But everything that we do know, tells us that we must tell them. Children value honesty above everything else. What they don't like are conspiracies of silence, withheld information, suppressed emotional expression and just generally being excluded in the interest of protecting them.

It sometimes seems preferable at the time to present the death as a tragic accident.

In Caitlin's case, I did just that. She had many young friends for whom she babysat, and who loved her, and my first test came not long after her death when I was having a cup of tea with close friends. Had Caitlin lived she would have been spending the summer before her first term at university with this family in the south of France looking after Max, then seven, and Sophie, then three. Max didn't mince his words: 'Why did she die?'

'She was very ill,' I said (and as I spoke I flashed back to the inquest, where the stark conclusion was 'Caitlin Hurcombe killed herself', she was a 'healthy well-nourished' person . . . the only substance in her body was a 'therapeutic dose of fluoxetine hydrochloride'). Then came the thunderbolt from Max:

'How did she die?'

'It was very sudden,' I said. 'She just died.'

Max didn't ask any more questions, so perhaps it was enough at the time – not least because these questions came when we were sitting in the garden with his parents and grandmother, who remained silent during this conversation. I felt under excruciating pressure to protect my young listeners. I've learned since that presenting the tragedy of suicide as an accident or the result of sudden illness is not uncommon.

Margaret Harvey continues:

We do not want our children to glean from us that death is something that you can choose, that you can inflict it upon yourself. It runs contrary to all our protective instincts; we teach our children to stay alive and perhaps, deep down, we fear that if we talk to our children about suicide, we are somehow making it a possibility, a thing that they might even try for themselves.

The problem is that lies create secrets, and family secrets are on the whole very bad for health. We've held back something, know something, that they do not know.

The parameters discussed in Chapter 3 hold true for suicide and, for that matter, with other 'unnatural deaths' – in other words, that we explain within the bounds of age and understanding. Honest answers to questions are then part of the family tapestry.

Margaret Harvey suggests some words we might use, although she points out correctly that each parent must find his or her own way 'through the nightmare':

> As with all talk about death, we need to follow our children's lead, to listen carefully to the questions they are asking. Once they understand that their brother or sister is dead, the probable next question (from a child old enough to ask) is 'How did they die?' This is the first point at which we have to take a deep breath and say what actually happened: she took too many tablets, he put a rope around his neck and it choked him, he fell off the bridge. The difficulty is often in saying enough, but not too much; we need to listen, wait for the next question, and not get bogged down in the motivation aspect until it arises. We try to avoid giving graphic detail, the stuff of nightmares, but also not to say anything that they will later find out to have been untrue. Children of junior school age are often obsessed with the practical detail and their imaginings are usually much worse than the facts – so having the facts, straight answers to specific questions, helps to control their imagination. But each of us has to judge how much, and when.

It's when the 'why' question comes up that things get even harder, not least because most of us don't know, and some of us never will know, the answer to this heart-wrenching question. Margaret Harvey calls on personal experience:

> Some of our children were suffering from depression . . . perhaps they were on medication. They had, for want of a better way to say it, a 'mind sickness'. I personally feel resistant to explaining all suicide as illness, but I can see that it is one way that a child can begin to get hold of the reality. They may have been aware of their brother's mood swings, of his sadness, of the days he could

not get out of bed; it helps to connect these up to the illness and to his death. The other main road is that of the 'impulsive act': the exhaust hose in the car after a break-up ... or you have failed your exams which drives you to jump off a bridge. And here we need to give very clear messages: we think this was what happened, but how sad we are that he could not get help, because there was help there if only he had been able to ask for it. I think it is not appropriate to tell a young child 'he did not want to live any more'; that is too abstract a thought, for they themselves do not think about living, it is something that they *do*.

We do need to emphasize that there is always ... help, that nothing is so bad that there is no solution. It may seem like that for a time, but that is why we need friends and families, why we try to look after each other. But we do have to ask, to tell people when things are bad, so they can help us. If we can get that message across, we have helped to communicate a valuable thought for the rest of ... [our children's] lives. Children need reassurance that the death was not their fault, that nothing they said or did caused what happened. It seems obvious to us, but at a certain stage of development children do often think that their thoughts can cause things to happen. And they also need to be relieved of the burden of thinking that if they had been different, then they could have prevented it. The feeling 'Didn't she love me enough to stay alive?' will probably need talking about at some stage, but it is another quite abstract thought that may come later. Our surviving children need not be burdened with guilt for something that was not their fault ... we want our children to know that we think their brother or sister could have been helped if the circumstances had been different, and that taking your own life is never the best solution, however terrible the problem. We do not blame our dead child for what happened, but we wish with all our heart that their story could have had a different ending.

Sex and social pressures

Relationship difficulties are often implicated in suicide attempts among the young – over half (52 per cent) of adolescents who took an overdose in one study reported having problems with a boyfriend or girlfriend. The underlying causes of unhappiness are likely to be more profound than this, but vulnerable young people clearly experience acute stress when their relationships go wrong. Sexual intimacy raises the emotional stakes exponentially, and makes rejection much worse.

The 'Old Fogey police' will be on my case for the thoughts that follow, but that's too bad. Earlier sexual activity has exposed young people to the emotional and physical risks of sex as well as its pleasures. The sexual revolution of the 1960s, brought about by more permissive social mores and the arrival of the contraceptive pill, separated sex from the necessity of marriage and the fear of conception. Premarital sex became more common and young people began sexual relationships at an earlier age. The 'guesstimate' age for loss of virginity is now said to be 15 (I conducted my own straw poll by asking 20 of Caitlin's college friends, male and female, when they became 'non-virgins', and consensus produced the same age – 15). One young man recalled that 'at around 14 or 15 there was all this emphasis on "shagging". It was expected that you really wanted to "do it".' This isn't to say that casual sex is the norm, but neither are long-term involvements. Much more often, teens have intense short-term relationships which may cause pain when they end.

Our family has certainly had personal experience of the pressures I'm talking about. After a traumatic and protracted separation and divorce, I moved to a small rural community with Caitlin and my partner; Caitlin's older brother Sean was by now living independently in London. Caitlin made friends quickly and easily; she had a pony called Julie, and said she liked living out in the country. She also visited her father regularly in London.

Not long into her first term at the local school she came home crying.

'Darling, what's wrong?'

'They laughed at me in science today, Mum.'

'Why?'

'One of the boys shouted out in front of everybody, "Hey, Caitlin, do you do threesomes with your mum?" And everybody just laughed at me. The teacher didn't do anything except tell everyone to settle down – she was laughing too.'

Then she said, 'Mum, what's a threesome?'

I tried to explain what I understand to be a threesome, and also to let her know that this boy, whoever he was, was totally out of order. I was cut to the heart on her behalf. She was happy for me to see her teacher and the principal of the school to sort things out. The school responded quickly and skilfully, and that was that. Except that it wasn't. It turned out that even at the ages of 13 and 14, Caitlin was being challenged by her peers. 'C'mon, prove you're not a lezzie' was the gist. Contrary to my first defensive assumptions, Caitlin wasn't being singled out in this way; her friends from traditional and solo-parent homes got similar taunting.

We signed up for family counselling so that we could, for want of a better term, normalize our new life together and, for my part, find out how to be a better parent to Caitlin now we weren't together as a traditional family. Since my life companion is now female, I also wanted Caitlin to be reassured that she was a normal young girl. She had her own proper personal counsellor throughout, and the report at the end described Caitlin as a healthy, confident, balanced feisty girl whose developing sexuality was entirely normal. We found the counsellors affirming and extremely helpful.

Both Caitlin and her friends continued to be subjected to pressure from her male peer group about having sex. This, I learned later, was characteristic of a crude attitude in our area that 'if there's grass on the pitch, the game's on'. How widespread the attitude is, I don't know, but this pressure, unsavoury as it is, was echoed by her older brother's girlfriend of the time, then in her early twenties, who said Caitlin should sleep with as many boys as she could. Nobody seemed to ask her what *she* wanted.

Feelings of guilt and suicide

When someone we love intentionally takes their own life, their death is an ultimate and irretrievable message of despair. Many would say that it is an aggressive act, the ultimate revenge. And perhaps sometimes suicide can be the inverse of hatred, anger turned against oneself (Alvarez, 1971). Dr Edwin Schneidman (1984), author of numerous books on suicide, wrote: 'I believe that the person who commits suicide puts his psychological skeleton in the survivor's emotional closet – he sentences the survivor to deal with many negative feelings and, more, to become obsessed with thoughts regarding his own actual or possible role in having precipitated the suicidal act or having failed to abort it.'

It is extremely difficult to avoid feeling that to some degree we were responsible – Why didn't I ring back? Why did I get so angry?

Why didn't I stay with her instead of going to work? Why did I let him go off that weekend in the middle of an argument? And what if we *were* responsible? What if they say it was our fault? Unfortunately they are not around to have a debate about the other predisposing factors in the parts of their life that did not include us. The only reason to feel guilty is if we set up our loved one to die by suicide. And, hard as it sounds, the 'if onlys' of the past aren't going to help any of us.

Impact on the family

Each suicide has its own story that the family must attempt to unravel. None of us is ever prepared for the suicide of our child, whatever the circumstances surrounding the death. Even for those families who have lived for years with a child's mental health problems, repeated attempts at self-destruction and inability to believe that the future might be better, the actual death is still a profound shock. For some parents there is no such introduction; the suicide comes out of the blue, and the police are at the door telling you something you cannot begin to absorb.

Some of us may not have seen our child for months or years, while the lives of others of us were closely entwined and our child lived, and even died, in the family home. The common threads are the feelings: numbness, shock, disbelief, and then the questions. And all this is before the pain of grief and loss truly begins.

Suicide brings added complications to bereaved families. Although thankfully it is no longer regarded as a criminal or sinful act, some families do discover how difficult it can be to talk openly about suicide, how uncomfortable even close friends can feel about the tragedy, and how this can lead to isolation. There can also be differences, as well as togetherness, even within the immediate family in the way each person views the past as well as in their interpretation of the death. These differences can be very divisive. Misunderstandings can grow as each parent pursues a disparate road. Rifts can widen and real estrangement can occur, even between partners who previously thought themselves to be close. Marriages and partnerships become highly vulnerable, and can and do break down in the aftermath of the death of a child for any reason, and suicidal deaths compound the dangers.

Recently a dear friend, a brilliant designer and mother of two young children, suffered a devastating major stroke which paralysed her left side. She told me that the surgeons described strokes as an 'insult to the brain'. Like a stroke, suicide is an insult, to the soul rather than the brain – both the soul of the person who died by their own hand, and of the people who loved them.

Critical stigma

Michael Dunn (2000) raises an important issue for survivors of suicide:

> One unfortunate aspect of bereavement following suicide is that research has shown that there may be ill-feeling from others towards us: there may be some disquiet, similar to our own, that we must have contributed to the death in some way. There's nothing we can do about this except to be more alert in the future to others' needs who might be in our situation.

A good example of being somehow 'marked' by others after suicide was a direct comment from a parent of one of Caitlin's college friends. With support from Caitlin's teacher and from the brilliant actor Pete Postlethwaite, I founded a scholarship in Caitlin's memory, called Caitlin's Kickstart Award, to benefit students from our rural community who were unable to continue their formal studies as a result of the government's change from the grant to a loan system for further/higher education. The comment was, 'Don't you think you are in danger of glorifying your daughter and the way she died by doing this?' I responded with gape-mouthed silence, but wish I'd reminded her that there have been many times, like in unjust wars, where we fear our children may have died in vain, but that this does not make it a bad idea to remember and honour their lives.

Caitlin

My daughter Caitlin was an optimist; she wanted to be a lawyer and a singer and a film star, all at once. After a brief patch of bullying in middle school, she stood up for herself, as did her friends and teachers, and Mum and partner too, and came out the other side stronger and feistier. She grew up believing that teachers and electricians and doctors and gardeners and lawyers, plumbers and politicians are mainly pretty good people. We talked about this, we two optimists – people on the whole, we agreed, prefer the buzz of helping others than the buzz of doing harm. Those who didn't come from our 'take' on life were the sad people on Oprah and Ricki Lake and Jerry Springer, the talk shows and tabloids and shocking television documentaries – the *not-us* people. Caitlin also demanded high standards of me as a parent that I couldn't always meet, most dramatically in the failure of my marriage to the father she adored unconditionally.

Her suicide brought me to the flip side of this rosy picture. After her death, at the inquest, I heard evidence that Caitlin had only one substance in her body at the time of her death: a therapeutic dose of her prescription medication.

This hard fact sent me obtaining all her medical records, and to study statistics on drugs and suicide, not only the illegal 'recreational' sort, but alcohol, and over-the-counter and prescription drugs. Did records exist of suicides occurring when taking a drug (legal or otherwise) and/or in an alcohol-free situation? Colin Murray Parkes (Brown and Ferguson-Brown, 2001), one of our most highly respected bereavement experts, has stated that most suicides will contain drugs in the equation, either illegal, alcohol or medication-related. But, far as I know, no extensive figures are yet available. It is simply presumed that people want to kill themselves, and then find the way of doing it. But could it be this simple? I then put a notice in two specialist publications, asking that bereaved families contact me if their children died by suicide while taking drugs, stating a specific interest in antidepressant medication. My request yielded many replies, and what has evolved is a national self-help group for people suffering from medication-related adverse/violent/suicidal reactions (see Helpful Contacts).

We bereaved parents can deal with 'hows' if we can investigate the 'whys'. We will leave no stone unturned. The trail doesn't always lead anywhere, as it has in Caitlin's case, and looking back many of us will conclude that the things we don't know about the death of our child will always be infinitely more difficult to deal with than the things we do know. We may never discover the answer, but I would not discourage anyone from going down the 'why' road – with the following caveat. Knowing *why* changes nothing – our child is dead and will never come back on this earth – and in that sense our search is not 'helpful'. At the time of writing, serious dangers – including blunted emotions, violence, murder and suicide – are reliably connected to the taking of certain drugs in susceptible individuals. Two SSRI antidepressants, paroxetine (Seroxat) and venlafaxine (Efexor), are now banned for the treatment of depression in people under 18 because of demonstrated risks of violence and suicidal ideation.

The drug companies would no doubt claim that depressed people are more likely to kill themselves, that Caitlin had undiagnosed depression and that unfortunately the drug didn't prevent her taking her life. Were she alive, she'd retort that she simply wanted this type of drug because she believed what the ads said and what 'everyone' else was saying about it – its much-lauded feel-good factor and slimming properties as much as anything; all she had to do to obtain the drug was say the right words to a well-meaning doctor. It took her just seven minutes to do so.

In 2002 I served as consultant and participant with four national television programmes in England and Wales, and was invited to the United States in October 2002 to make a presentation at a ground-breaking medical-legal conference, cheerlessly but accurately titled 'SSRI Drugs: Suicide, Homicide, Seizures, Dependency'. It became apparent when Caitlin's individual story fell into context, that to the big companies, whose budgets are the envy of many a developed country, one teen 'consumer' called Caitlin Elizabeth Rosalie Hurcombe is a blip, collateral damage in a marketing strategy, her story 'anecdotal' and therefore of dubious reliability.

Forgiveness

I'm thinking about a play from my high school days by Thornton Wilder called *The Angel Who Troubled the Waters*. I remember just one scene and virtually nothing else about the plot. The crucifixion has happened. Jesus descends into hell, as he does in one version of the Apostles' Creed ('For our sake he was crucified under Pontius Pilate; he descended into hell. On the third day he rose again in fulfilment of the scriptures . . .'). In Wilder's play, Jesus literally goes to hell because he has to find Judas, forgive him, and take him to Paradise. Judas, you'll remember, betrayed Jesus for 30 pieces of silver and sent him off to be killed by his own people. Then, after trying and failing to return the blood money he'd accepted, Judas hanged himself in despair. But Jesus finds him and says, 'Not your fault, Judas, you were a pawn of history. Come with me.' Now, whatever your theology or lack thereof, this is impressive forgiveness.

A tale of modern forgiveness comes from Enniskillen (Wilson and McCreary, 1990), in this case murder rather than suicide, but relevant to this discussion. On Sunday, 8 November 1987, Remembrance Sunday, in Enniskillen in Northern Ireland, Gordon Wilson and his daughter Marie, a young nurse, arrived at the Cenotaph to remember the dead. An IRA bomb exploded. Gordon and Marie took a direct hit from the blast. Gordon survived his serious injuries, but Marie was killed. The following morning he was interviewed for a news report:

> The wall collapsed . . . and we were thrown forward . . . rubble and stones . . . all around us and under us. I remember thinking . . . 'I'm not hurt' . . . but there's a pain in my shoulder . . . I shouted to Marie, 'Are you all right?' and she said, 'Yes' . . . She found my hand and said, 'Is that your hand, Dad?' . . . I said 'Are you all right, dear?' . . . but we were under six feet of rubble . . . three or four times I asked her . . . she always said, 'Yes, I'm all right . . . ' I asked her the fifth time . . . 'Are you all right, Marie?' . . . She said, 'Daddy, I love you very much . . . ' Those were the last words she spoke to me . . . I kept shouting, 'Marie, are you all right?' . . . There was no reply. I have lost my daughter, but I bear no ill will, I bear no grudge . . . Dirty sort of talk is not going to bring her back to life . . . I don't have an answer . . . But I know there has to be a plan. If I didn't think that, I would commit suicide . . . It's part of a greater plan, and God is good . . . And we shall meet again.

In a few broken sentences, Gordon Wilson somehow said it all for the bereaved, the injured and the suffering, as well as for those who suffered with and through him. His words entered the collective memories of millions. Gordon Wilson described himself as a simple man, and stood by his first shocked, heartbroken statement. He has spent the years following Enniskillen working in his quiet way for the elimination of hatred and misunderstanding.

Support following the suicide of a loved one

There are many support agencies for grieving families – from highly structured courses in 'grief recovery', where tuition-paying bereaved students receive a diploma at the end of the course (as in 'I've just graduated from Grief University International'?), to personal talking therapy and counselling programmes tailored to individual needs.

Isolation

For those of us who crave isolation following the loss of a child to suicide, the continued mantra of contact with others may be quite dismaying. Do we truly want to be comforted? Are we not now men and women of sorrow and acquainted with grief? Is our grief not our only real contact with our child? And is it not sometimes a good idea to spare others when the heavy rocks weigh us down too much to hide? The jury is out on this one, beyond reflecting that being alone in the company of those who understand and care can be a life-saver. Charlie Walton, in *When There Are No Words* (Walton, 1996), writes:

> Don't let your pride convince you that you need to be independent and never beholden to anyone. You will go through this alone ... but you'll go through it alone better if you let people help. It will help you and it will help them if you can give *the gift of asking*. People need to do things and you ... need to let them.
>
> When our boys died and a little group of us sat in our den and watched the morning turn from darkness to daylight, Bud finally said, 'I'm cooking breakfast.' I had known Bud for twenty-eight years and had never known him to cook anything except a shrewd business deal. Bud was the last person in the house that any of us would have nominated to cook breakfast. And ... while there may have been a few expressions of amazement ... there was not one person who questioned the sentiment. Bud needed to *do* something ... anything ... that felt like it was for Charlie and Kay and Bob and Carole.
>
> When people come to you and say, 'If there's anything we can do, please call on us,' listen to their offers as sincerely as they are making them. They really want to do something. They can't explain the thing that is hurting you so much but they would

sincerely love to do something . . . anything . . . that feels like it is for you.

Let them do things for you. Don't burden yourself trying to be creative in thinking up clever little jobs to keep all your friends occupied with busy work. Your primary job is to get yourself through this time of loss. Take care of yourself first. But when you do think of little jobs that need to be tended to and people that need to be contacted, take your friends up on their offers to help. They asked. They meant it. Let them do it.

The suicide note

The idea that a person might choose to die is at odds with our dearest belief that all human life is beyond price and sacred. Suicide seems to cock a snook at the very notion of the intrinsic value of life. The following 'farewell' letter comes from a gifted 22-year-old called David. In granting permission for its publication, David's family hope that the loved ones of people who die by suicide might find some comfort in his words, and hopefully a greater understanding of mental illness:

Dear Mom, Dad and Stephany
First some facts:

- I LOVE YOU VERY MUCH.
- I KNOW YOU LOVE ME VERY MUCH. If love alone could make me better, I would be the most well-adjusted man on earth. Please don't feel that you neglected to tell or show me how much you loved me.
- YOU WERE NOT TO BLAME FOR MY CONDITION. I believe my mental illness was a result of a chemical imbalance in the brain. A certain percentage of people from all types of family situations have a major mental illness. It was just the luck of the biological draw that I happened to be one of them. Whether it was major Depressive Disorder, Schizoid Personality Disorder, Manic Depressive Disorder more commonly called bipolar, or Schizophrenia, my mental illness made my life unliveable. But you are not to blame for that. So please don't let yourselves feel guilty.

– I KNOW THAT YOU WILL MAKE IT THROUGH THIS. It won't be easy, but you will have a lot of support from a lot of friends and relatives. Don't be like me, the ultimate schizoid loner. Count on the support of your friends and relatives.

If only you knew what goes on inside my head. I know you will say that I didn't try long enough or hard enough. I have been emotionally disturbed since late childhood. I now have a major mental illness. I tried as long and as hard as I could. I've had all sorts of suggestions, like: Repeat positive phrases over and over again. Don't eat foods with yeast. Take Haldol. Don't take Haldol. Accept Jesus as my personal saviour. Quit smoking, get a girlfriend. And the list goes on and on . . .

I know that the above suggestions were made with the best intentions, but they lack an understanding of what mental illness is all about. That's why I found something in common with other people who are mentally ill. When they told me how being mentally ill affects their lives, I understood, because my illness affected me in the same way.

If I were to tell Uncle Ray that I had bought a gun, that I felt suicidal, he would have no alternative but to call the hospital and the police and before you know it I'd be back in the hospital. I'd rather be dead. It's not like I killed myself because I didn't get an A on an exam, or because I broke up with my girlfriend. Those are the kinds of depression that have a reason to happen. My depression comes without any help from the outside. Nothing bad has happened to make me depressed except my depression.

It's not like I did this 'on a lark'. I've had over a year to think it over. But, I can hardly expect you to understand about something I myself don't understand. I don't know why I am the way I am. The man who didn't see it through. That is what this is. If given a chance to choose between an eternity in heaven or another go-round as a human on earth, I'm certain I would choose the latter. And now for the business part of this suicide note:

Cremate and scatter me (I don't care where).

All my money goes to you. Everything else, too. Do with it what you will. But may I suggest sending a portion of my worldly goods to a mental health research foundation of your choice. (*As requested, the family sent a donation to a mental health fund. I first published this note in the TCF newsletter, Summer 2001, issue 128.)*

David clearly did his best to alleviate his loved ones' guilt and pain and his note is very carefully constructed. It is a note that reflects his state of mind at the time the note was written, but it is unlikely that the essence of the tragedy can be prised from the suicide note, however lucid it appears.

David's tragic letter raises immense and unsolved questions about the nature of mental illness, the tangled equation of the 'nature versus nurture' debate, and the impossible waste of a young life snuffed out by his own hand, and which seems to have been based on the belief held by David (not a belief I share) – that his 'mental illness' resulted from a chemical imbalance in his brain.

What if David had been able to take his despair and turn it round? Young people who make the decision *not* to kill themselves almost seem to possess a mechanism or mechanisms to transform despair, self-hatred and rage into something positive. If we could bottle this mechanism, this *something*, maybe we could save many from the final cul-de-sac of self-immolation. For my part, I was grateful to Caitlin for writing a note.

Many writings of deepest despair exist, and the following anonymous poem was sent to me by my niece Rosanna after Caitlin died. The writer is not known, but the poem is attributed to a 12-year-old suffering from depression:

> The beauty of love has not found me
> Its hands have not gripped me so tight
> For the darkness of hate is upon me
> I see day, not as day, but as night.

> I yearn for the dear love to find me
> With my heart and my soul and my might
> For darkness has closed in upon me
> I see day, not as day, but as night.

The children are playing and laughing
But I cannot find love in delight
There is an iron fence all around me
I see day, not as day, but as night.

(Anonymous)

Eminent psychologist Dorothy Rowe, in her book *Depression: The Way Out of Your Prison* (Rowe, 2001), claims, based on her decades of counselling depressed people, that 'What determines our behaviour isn't what happens to us but how we interpret what happens to us. We have very little control over what happens to us, but we always have a choice about how we interpret what happens to us.' It may be possible, with courage and determination, to change these ideas. The novelist James Frey claims to have done just that. After years of self-destructive addiction to many toxic substances: 'I took all the force I used to destroy myself and used it to save myself. I found a way to channel the rage into something positive,' he writes.

Not long after Caitlin died a friend came to visit, and as she listened to my woeful tale and, especially at that time, my dread of the inquest, she nodded, 'Hmm-m, suicide, the ultimate revenge.' I read Caitlin's (totally non-vengeful) farewell note aloud. My friend told me that in her research only one in five people who die by suicide will leave a note. I was horrified at first, not least because, although I cannot honestly say I was comforted, I could say that Caitlin's farewell note had been as loving as it was filled with a sense of rejection and loss of control, and that I was grateful she'd written it. My friend's estimate of one in five is at the low end of the scale; other studies have revealed widely varying results. Just under half the 17 surviving loved ones interviewed in *A Special Scar* (Wertheimer, 2001) received a note or letter, but the average estimate falls somewhere between 25 per cent and 30 per cent.

The valley of the shadow of death

Whether we are left with a farewell message or not, it is true that many suicidal people are perfectionists who have been brought up to expect a great deal from life and who have been thwarted in their desire to be able to give it back. Sometimes they make unrealistic demands on themselves, wanting more than it is possible to obtain. A different set of rules seems to operate, often exacerbated by the models of perfection constantly bombarding them on all fronts.

Elly Hobbs, mother of Martin, tells the following story:

I had been a committed Christian for 45 years when our 29-year-old son, Martin, who was a very hard-working young doctor, took his life after taking the SSRI drug sertraline [also known as Lustral] for two to three days to treat his depression. This happened on 26 May 1995. I felt God had totally abandoned me and our family. All the promises in the Bible to those who love and serve the Lord were true for every other family except mine. I could not read or sing the twenty-third psalm, especially verse six – 'Surely goodness and mercy shall follow me all the days of my life' – without crying. I never lost my faith and I was never angry with God, but I just felt totally abandoned by the God whom I loved.

It was not until March 1996 when the Dunblane massacre* took place that, strangely, a small glimmer of light entered my darkness. I was watching a service from the cathedral where the Rector spoke about the massacre and all the messages of sympathy he had received. One message had made him very angry and he looked straight at me from the screen when he said that a lady had said to him, 'I do not understand the will of God,' and his reply was, 'This was not the will of God.' It was as if he said this to me about Martin's death. Later in the service a man sang the twenty-third psalm and when he came to the verse, 'Even though I walk through the valley of the shadow of death . . . your rod and your staff they comfort me,' I thought, 'Yes, but I do not know how to lay hold of that rod and staff.'

I continued to exist somehow until March 1997 when I was in Israel and visited Yad Vashem, the Holocaust Museum, for the third time. I found myself crying with the Jews all the way through, as I identified with them as they were stripped of everything, their clothes, their gold teeth, their jewellery, their dignity, and walked naked to the gas chambers. They must have found it unbelievable that their God, whom they had worshipped all their lives, would allow this to happen to them, and yet they went singing to their death, knowing that they had no one else to put their trust in but God. I felt that I had been stripped naked before God, that he had taken away from me everything that I had built my faith on, and there was nothing left but him. I could then begin to accept what had happened to my family and gradually I have come to a place where peace and pain lie down together.

But I will never be the person I was before my lovely son died. You do not go through such an experience without being changed for ever.

(*Dunblane: On 13 March 1996, Thomas Hamilton, a disgraced former Scout master, turned his guns on a class of five- and six-year-old children at Dunblane primary school. He shot dead 16 children and their teacher in three minutes of carnage in the primary school gym before killing himself. All but one of the 29 children in the class were killed or injured.)

Befriending

For Elly and for bereaved people everywhere who discover the resource and wish to tap it, there exists an entire culture of men, women and children who share feelings and aid one another's survival. 'Nowhere ... are these shared feelings more fully expressed than in the extraordinary and moving series of pamphlets and newsletters issued by The Compassionate Friends' (Albery *et al.*, 1997).

TCF is a befriending organization, and Margaret Hayworth has described befriending thus (Spring 1989):

We are all befrienders. We all share when we write a letter, make a phone call or talk with another bereaved parent at a meeting. We share when we read the newsletter ... The necessity to 'share' and talk about our loved ones ... is a need within all bereaved people that requires to be met ... Grief is a natural reaction to the death of a loved one/ones ... Befriending from the time of death may mean that counselling will be needed by a small minority only: those who become 'stuck' in their grief; who have other problems within their family; or difficulties within themselves due to past experiences. For these, bereavement counselling is very beneficial and ... complementary to befriending.

Suicide prevention

Suicides that do not happen do not provide data, and so the success or otherwise of suicide prevention is hard to prove.

In response to the huge rise in suicides in recent years, suicide prevention has been added to the already bulging 'Health' intray of the government. In 2002, suicide prevention was one of 600 Treasury efficiency and performance documents with a target of reducing the number of suicides by 17 per cent by the year 2010. Rather underwhelming, but better than nothing.

There are active organizations dedicated to preventing suicide: PAPYRUS (see Helpful Contacts at the back of the book) produces leaflets and holds conferences, as well as participating in the government's working paper on suicide prevention.

There are also talking therapies and programmes – unfortunately not widely available — that address the dangers of suicide specifically, not least the 12-step programmes and Cognitive Behavioural Therapy (see p. 144).

Suicidal intention: warning signs

- Talking about it. The common wisdom is that talking about suicide is the equivalent to crying wolf. Not true.
- Sudden changes in behaviour, either withdrawn or 'speedy', disruptive or violent.
- Taking unnecessary risks.
- Increased alcohol or drug intake.
- Changes in eating habits.
- 'Bunking off' school; decline in standards of school work.
- Ending of a relationship.
- Bereavement (can make someone very vulnerable if the death was by suicide).
- Self-harming.
- Despondency and loss of interest in life.
- Adverse reactions to medication, including intense agitation (akathesia), nightmares, emotional blunting, self-harm.

It goes without saying that it is too late for those of us bereaved by suicide to help our beloved children. As we live on, though, we may be able to help others. For a start, we can disabuse people of certain kinds of misinformation; for example:

- Those who think suicide is just an easy way out for cowards need to know that suicidal thoughts are not a respecter of persons. The reality is that all kinds of people, including those who appear to be strong, are vulnerable to killing themselves (Helen, 2002).

143

- Those who, including the more sympathetic among us, think that avoiding talk of suicide (when we're worried about a loved one's behaviour) is the best plan, should think again. Listening to/ talking to a trusted someone about suicidal despair can be life-saving.

Cognitive Behavioural Therapy (CBT)

CBT can be of benefit after a bereavement, for it 'has been shown to be as effective as antidepressants in the treatment of depression in a number of randomized trials' (Ratna, 2002). It can also be useful in helping people to overcome negative patterns of thinking that reinforce feeling bad, and behaving in ways that do not help.

7

You Are the Expert

'Grieving is like being lost,' she said.
'What is the difference between exploring and being lost?' he asked.
'Do you have a compass?' she said. 'I think that will help.'

(Linda Hurcombe)

I began editing the quarterly newsletter (more recently titled *Compassion*) of The Compassionate Friends (TCF) in the spring of 2001. Simon Stephens, at the time a hospital chaplain, founded TCF in 1969 with the help of two families. Over the years he has received many honours, including an OBE. In his acceptance speech for one award he said:

> [TCF] was born out of a gut reaction to the conspiracy of silence with which contemporary society . . . isolated bereaved parents . . . It is my sincere belief that with the grace of the Holy Spirit and the care of The Compassionate Friends, many bereaved parents have transformed their own bitter grief . . . a crown of thorns, into a victor's laurels.

TCF co-founder Joe Lawley continues (Clarke, 1998):

> On the 21st day of May 1968, an 11-year-old boy on his way to school was knocked from his bicycle by a van. His name was Kenneth Lawley. Within minutes he was admitted to the intensive care unit at the Coventry and Warwickshire Hospital. Elsewhere in that large hospital, another boy, Billy Henderson, lay seriously ill, in the terminal stages of cancer.
>
> Gathered round the bed of Kenneth were family and close friends who had come from all parts of the country to be with Iris and Joe, Kenneth's parents. Another who offered help, the young assistant hospital chaplain, Simon Stephens, stood back from the group. His offer of help was to be there all the time to talk, to listen, to pray. In his prayers over the bed of each boy he mentioned the other. Gradually through individual grief came the realization that another family at this time was experiencing the same pain, the same anguish.

Iris and Joe's minister and friend, the Revd David Dale, also had comforted Bill and Joan Henderson through the long anxious months when they nursed Billy virtually day and night. He came quickly from a conference to be with both families. In his prayers for their return to health, he too linked both boys and their families.

Tragically both boys died: Kenneth on the 23rd May, Billy shortly afterwards. The bedside vigil was over, both families returning home to a life without their beloved sons ... In an expression of understanding, Iris Lawley suggested that she and Joe send flowers to the funeral of Billy. Joan and Bill telephoned to thank them. They visited each other, they became friends. They spoke to each other about their sons. They helped each other because they knew how the others were feeling.

The Society of the Compassionate Friends (as originally titled) was officially established in January 1969 by six founder members who placed on record the Society's aim: 'To offer friendship and understanding to any person, irrespective of colour and creed, who finds himself or herself heartbroken and socially isolated by the death of a child.'

Some years later Joe Lawley recalled that in his prayers before Kenneth died, he had prayed, 'I'll do anything, I'll be a missionary, I'll give blood.' In the event, Joe, with Simon Stephens and the other parents, did become missionaries of a sort – for bereaved parents all over the world.

By 1971 Simon Stephens was travelling to the United States to help set up a chapter of TCF there. Over the ensuing decades TCF has spread round the world, with chapters in South Africa, the Netherlands, Malta, Spain, Australia, New Zealand, the United States, and many more countries.

What has The Compassionate Friends achieved? It is not immodest to say that it has led the way on an international scale to a change of attitude towards child bereavement. By giving voice to and supporting people's descriptions of what it is like to go through such loss, literally 'giving sorrow words' with someone to listen, and repeatedly affirming both the complexity and the authenticity of members' experience, TCF has brought healing and growth to countless people around the world.

Today, TCF UK publishes an impressive body of literature to help bereaved parents in a variety of situations, including anthologies of parents' writings and past articles from the newsletter that have continuing relevance. The leaflets subcommittee has evolved a dynamic process of team writing, which prepares materials by canvassing as many bereaved people in given specific areas – for example, 'The Sudden Death of Our Child', 'Coping with Special Occasions', 'When Your Child has Died Abroad' – and then publishing cooperatively produced pamphlets that are periodically updated.

The TCF logo was designed by John Fisher and first used in 1975:

John and Maggie Fisher lost their daughter Clare when she was eight years old. John wrote:

> By chance we met someone, who knew someone, who had heard of The Compassionate Friends, who lived ... some 20 or 30 miles from our home, and as a consequence Mrs Joan Wills wrote to us and subsequently came to our home ... Although we still feel our loss greatly, we both know that we are now ready to assist the Friends (as TCF was then commonly called) ourselves. Our help would also include the services of my own company (John Fisher Design & Marketing Ltd), which include advertising, design, marketing and public relations activities ... We are mobile, immediately available, and ready, both physically and spiritually, to begin work for the Friends. Please use us.

At the time the logo was bright emerald green, but has subsequently settled into the present UK flagship colour of royal blue.

I spoke with John Fisher, and he shared with me a moving anecdote about the logo when it was in design stage. John was describing the logo design for TCF National Committee approval.

One of the committee members was blind, and John was explaining the design 'as a virtual visual picture'. He described a circle with hands moving to touch in the foreground – on the background, a road-like grid moving upwards and towards the stylized featureless figure of a child walking away up the road at the top of the logo. The unsighted colleague asked simply, 'How do you know the child is moving away from you?'

TCF friends in the United States have said this of John Fisher's design:

> Much of the beauty of our logo lies in the fact that there are no definitive answers to its symbolism. At first glance the meaning seems obvious; yet as one looks more closely, questions may arise. The hands represent different things to us at different periods in our grief journeys. To the newly bereaved, the hands reach out, offering comfort and support. Later in our grief . . . they may symbolize the process of . . . coming to terms with our child's death. Still later . . . we begin to reach out towards others. Then *our* hands become the hands which are extended to newly bereaved people. The circle is complete: a circle of friends, a circle of love and understanding, with the child at the centre.

My editorial predecessor Pat Neil piloted the TCF newsletter for eight years (1993–2001), making her the longest-serving editor in TCF's history; it is to Pat that I owe a huge debt of inspiration for:

- Helping me to emerge from my shell to connect with other bereaved parents via the necessary correspondence involved in editing the newsletter, now titled *Compassion: The Quarterly Journal of TCF*.
- Continuing with this book. Writing books is a delicious but solitary occupation. The object in this case is altruistic, but the process of writing is highly introverted and, in the case of the subject matter, very painful. Most working time brings quiet tears.

Pat Neil has helped me to see that the isolation I so craved after losing Caitlin was not helpful. I had wanted to disconnect from friends, indeed from everyone, because I most unfairly projected my daughter's death into their eyes, and the maternal part of me, which is admittedly pretty substantial, wanted to protect them from my pain too. This was possibly understandable, but it didn't work.

I now realize that, had I gone on in this vein, not only would I have lost the possibility of creating something positive from the irreversible pain of lost love that was my initial 'inheritance', but that I might also have cauterized my own capacity to feel love again.

I discovered TCF just a year and a bit after Caitlin's death. I found people who do understand. Although there was no local contact group near me, I discovered a library with books I could devour, written by people who knew what I was going through. Some time later, through editing the journal, I rediscovered the importance of writing down words of love for our children, ourselves and one another, something that as a teacher and practitioner I had taken for granted in earlier years.

Of the importance of writing, Charlie Walton says (Walton, 2003):

> I have been amazed through the years that people, way back in elementary school, traumatized ... into thinking that they could never write anything ... will suddenly produce beautiful poems and other written sentiments in the process of remembering their children. There is something therapeutic about putting things on paper ... reading them over ... changing a word here and there, that really helps to focus the mind and get some of those inner feelings out where we can deal with them more effectively ... Writing doesn't necessarily work for everybody, but maybe pulling things out of your weary mind and on to a defenceless piece of paper can work for you.

Each person in TCF has lost at least one child, or sister or brother or grandchild. We are a circle of witnesses to living and growing through grief, and we are here to reach out and help one another. Had we not loved so much, we would not hurt so much. Had we not hurt so much, we would not be in need of healing.

Talking therapies: some advantages

My gran always said that if you cry too often on your friends' shoulders you won't have any friends left! And indeed, it can feel like a no-win situation with acquaintances: if you're coping, they think you don't care; if you don't cope, they think 'isn't it a shame they just can't cope'.

In the refuge of skilled therapy, there will be a safe oasis to cry plenty, and laugh too. Here's another unfashionable proposition: professional help can be very valuable. Former normative approaches to grief, based on a prescribed period of mourning and the idea that someone should have 'moved on' after that length of time, are on the whole now seen to be unhelpful. A good portion of professional guidance can focus on helping the grieving person to build a bond with the child who has died. It is crucial to bring death into the conversation about living.

If you find the right person, it is easier to share deepest concerns more readily, knowing that you won't be rejected or judged. Your carefully chosen counsellor will be familiar with grief and possibly help to bring important insights:

- Have you ever felt like this before?
- Did you feel like this when your mother/father/sibling/friend died? Childhood loss makes later loss worse.

If you do choose therapy, find a good counsellor who:

- can help unlock a cupboard of memories in a safe place, and can respect you when you do not wish to open certain cupboards;
- can help set limits, make targets, and find new ways of thinking about solutions to problems;
- will treat you with the respect you deserve, and help you to re-learn the world;
- can help you realize that grief is normal, that stopping grieving is OK too, and that shared grief can help.

Whatever path you explore in the territory of grief, your 'tasks of mourning' will continue:

- To accept the reality of your loss.
- To experience the pain of grief. Remember the song? 'It's so high, you can't get over it, so low, you can't get under it, so wide, you can't get around it, you must go in at the door.'
- To adjust to being in a place where the dead loved one is missing, and learning how to fill the void.
- To channel emotional energy and reinvest it in other activities. Take care of yourself. Develop a new relationship with your dead loved one. Thomas Campbell spoke for our children when he said: 'To live in hearts we leave behind is not to die.'

A *land of listeners*

Developing contacts and relationships is important and takes great strength; a solitary understanding of our child's death is not enough. We want others to know, to comprehend, to listen without judging, and we need *to be believed* – to have a safe place where what has happened to our children and those who love them may find a home and resting place. I have a stark example of the importance of listening, a time when I made a huge mistake. Although it doesn't concern the loss of a child, it formed for me an important life lesson about non-judgemental listening:

I had a university room-mate for a short time called Mary Louise, a laconic person who quickly became a laughing stock of the freshman class (mainly behind her back) because she kept repeating a weird story. She hailed from a place in East Tennessee called Oak Ridge, a new town (even by US standards) whose business involved military and NASA research. Mary Louise's parents worked in top secret occupations. What made Mary Louise a laughing stock was this: she claimed that at Oak Ridge they experimented on uninformed people as guinea pigs with radiation in the interests of the space programme and planning in the event of a nuclear disaster. She claimed that a relative of hers had died of radiation poisoning following an experiment. She said none of us was safe. I remember telling her not to be unpatriotic – we quite simply didn't believe her. Mary Louise left university soon after, and we didn't keep in contact. I heard that she'd suffered a breakdown. I am not happy with the way I treated Mary Louise. I should have listened – not least because, apparently, she was telling the truth.

The *unique fingerprint of grief*

I look at my hand and see five fingers, a palm, knuckles. It is like yours, this hand, but my fingerprint is unique to me. Grief, as discussed earlier, is like a fingerprint on a hand that is largely similar to all hands, a hand reaching out to hold, to bear, to support.

In grieving our dead child we have travelled to the heart of human suffering. 'We are, and what we are, suffers,' says J.B., in Archibald MacLeish's wondrous re-working of the book of Job. Can we find a way to redeem suffering? To turn it into music, create a precious oil and terrible beauty for healing? It does seem clear that sufferers who turn into witness-survivors become very good earth-shakers. I think of Aldous Huxley, writing *Island* while he tended to his wife on her deathbed, about the relationship of suffering to art – would there be art at all if we could eliminate human suffering?

The need for self-forgiveness

And how to face up to myself and forgive? It is very undignified to admit to being wrong, to lose face. Much easier to blame others, especially since they have lots and lots of faults, so no problem finding good reasons for it being their fault.

But if we can't see when we've done wrong, how do we make things right? How do we heal? How do we accept forgiveness and forgive others? These are common problems after the death of our child, too often unspoken, but gnawing away. If we can face up to the wrong things we have done, they will have less dominion over us. We can admit where we're wrong, and ask forgiveness. Memories that hurt – when our baby wouldn't stop crying and we were in danger of becoming a child batterer, when we shouted unnecessarily, didn't listen, broke promises, embarrassed or even humiliated him/her – these are human failings for which we must forgive ourselves. Where guilt and remorse dwell, dwells the solution of forgiveness, and with forgiveness dwells hope and love and faith and freedom.

A misery shared is a misery multiplied?

This statement from my granny represents as neatly as any I've come across the divide between the 'stiff upper lip' mentality that dominated some twentieth-century bereavement methods and thinking, and the more recent affirmation that sharing and carrying can lead to the creation of lasting bonds with our dead child, and lasting friendships that spring up between families and loved ones. We are all connected.

My granny also used to say, 'Don't wallow – wallowing's for pigs,' and indeed I know many grievers who find the peer counselling of TCF and the national conferences or 'gatherings' far too sad and woeful. Basically, it's 'horses for courses'. Whichever route the griever takes is a route of sadness, but one thing's for sure: we don't stand still.

Others say, particularly those who are critical of our counselling culture, that the pendulum has swung too far. Certainly, recent disasters witness to droves of volunteers, professionals and counsellors arriving at the unspeakable Dunblanes, Lockerbies, Columbines and 9/11s in the hope of fending off post-traumatic shock syndrome and all the other 'post-' syndromes connected to the catastrophes plaguing society. We live in a very cruel and dangerous world, but is it more so than in the past?

So is there any evidence that this trauma counselling is helpful? Perhaps not always, but on balance the answer is yes. Organizations like TCF have helped multitudes of grieving people, but they are not everyone's 'cup of tea'. 'How can you dwell on such sadness all the time?' some say to me – meaning well because they love me. 'Close that chapter of your life,' they say, meaning, I think, 'Stop dwelling on Caitlin's death.' They remind me that their 'father/mother/uncle/cousin did just that – after the funeral that was it, they just got on with their lives.' Or I am told about how the nuns in a convent with an ageing population allow themselves precisely one month to grieve a dead fellow sister. And I say to them, 'But this was my child, and I am, we are, getting on with our lives, in our own way.'

The simple fact is that grief isn't like the chapter of a book, or a door, or one room in a house – or even an amputation – for people who have lost a child. And everybody's individual circumstances will have a bearing. For example, experiences of grief in childhood often leads to more intense experiences of grief when bereavement occurs again. It is also true that the more we love, the more hard the grief. But who would stop loving because of this? It is certainly true that if grief cripples you, you are likely to need a crutch. We are still in the process of understanding the many, many faces of grief, and I suspect that the process will continue for a very long time.

I am often asked by the people I care about, 'How long do you intend to carry on with such all-encompassing work for no pay?' (A valid issue since – like most people – I need to earn my living, but find in my active senior years that the things I'm most passionate about tend to be at the 'nil' end of money-spinning occupations.) The answer is, 'For as long as it feels right to do so.' I have been a campaigner from way back – anti-war activities, pro-civil rights, a founder member of MOW (Movement for the Ordination of Women), Greenham Common, Amnesty International, Christian Aid, Greenpeace, Earthwatch, and so on – and I've found that this 'Linda on a mission' bit of me is something that has survived Caitlin's death and remains unchanged.

It is here, I believe, that TCF and its sister organizations have found a process, or processes, of 'being there' for fellow bereaved people, of helping us find strength. From the impossible early weeks of raw grief when there is no means of 'controlling' anything, to the months when those who held me in the first days must indeed get on with their lives and be elsewhere, TCF has built a safe house for growing through the living that goes on after death. I think of the wonderful motto of Christian Aid: 'We believe in life before death'. TCF believes in life *after* the death of a child, life that can grow to incorporate rather than forget, to give expression to, rather than silence, the fact that someone precious lived and that her/his life continues to bring beauty to this world in however modest a way. I've seen it again and again, and I admit that I'm trying to do exactly that.

TCF helps bereaved and grieving people become strong enough to live after the loss of their children. Subsequently many grow away to take part in other activities, perhaps to form other charities (often related to the way their child died). It is wonderful to see people 'moving forward'. However, TCF's greatest strength is those who, having been helped through their experiences, become strong enough themselves to provide the same kind of emotional support for those more recently bereaved – the idea that 'If I reach out to you now while you are weak, perhaps some day you will find strength to support another.'

Grief recovery programmes

Professionals in the area of bereavement have traditionally tried to create universal timetables for the grieving process; we may well hear 'two years' quoted in terms of 'recovery', or 'three years'. Some of us will be desperate to know the answer to our cry from the heart, '*When* will I stop feeling this way?' People's responses vary hugely, but, on the whole, more than four or five years of grieving – experts may differ on the actual length of time – and we may be said to be at risk of our grief becoming 'stuck', or even 'pathological' ('pathological' meaning 'diseased').

The dominant counselling and treatment model of the last half of the twentieth century held that the chief function of grief and mourning was a cutting of bonds with the dead person, an achievement of 'closure', of 'completion' and 'recovery'. These virtues are contrasted with their opposites, 'isolation' and 'avoidance', and incompleteness. Grievers were advised to follow a step-by-step plan to achieve successful recovery from grief and loss in order to be able to reinvest in new relationships in the present and with the living.

A variety of such grief recovery programmes existed – and indeed continue to thrive – based on this method of dealing with grief. *The Grief Recovery Handbook* (James and Friedman, 1998) represents a reliable and much-advocated example of this genre. However, there is a slightly worrying warning in the book's introduction which tells readers that they must not take the reading of the book as preparation to help others, which rather calls into question what the actual value of the book is. In fairness, it is likely that the authors are simply stressing the difference between reading about a programme and undertaking to teach it. To use a marine metaphor, they are protecting their seaworthy craft in an ocean of counselling that is sadly populated by many more sharks than dolphins.

Grief recovery programmes take students through various schedules of grief and cover the stages that the bereaved person is likely to live through. The concept of grief is expanded to include all kinds of loss – of a spouse, parent, child or pet, and other 'loss experiences', such as moving, starting school, recovery from illness, diagnosis of illness, retirement, economic change of fortune, holidays, legal problems, children growing up, etc. In the last stage of James and Friedman's course, students compose 'The Grief Recovery Completion Letter', in which they 'say goodbye' to their grief, and think of new opportunities for a fulfilled life. They then 'graduate' to live a new resolved life without their loved one, receiving a 'diploma' for their successful efforts.

Popular as they are, such rigid models are not for everyone. Many of us who have been bereaved for a number of years are aware that we have not 'got over' the death of our child in the expected 'two or three years'. In fact, we may never 'get over' our child's death at all – rather, we discover, almost breath by breath, how to re-learn and eventually to re-join life, to re-discover what 'normal' is again: a new 'normal' that is different from the time our child was with us, but a life based on continued bonds (Klass *et al.*, 1996) with our dead loved one.

Some people, though, do shut out loss with seeming success. One friend, Annette, lost a much-wanted baby born still at full term. In addition to chaplaincy baptismal services, the hospital offered a skilled counselling programme which included the opportunity to dress the baby, hold and name her, to take photographs, to have a formal funeral. Annette's husband Adrian, as well as the grandparents, were keen to have these mementos, but Annette wanted nothing to do with it. As far as she was concerned, the baby was dead and the best thing to do was to get on with life. I am grossly oversimplifying here, but it is necessary to respect Annette's stoical response to such loss. And indeed, Annette and Adrian did 'pick up the pieces' and went on to have a healthy baby who is the apple of their eye. I am full of admiration for Annette's courage, but admit that I don't begin to understand it. Yet again, it's a demonstration of our diversity: just because most parents will be glad to have seen and held their dead newborn baby does not mean that everyone must feel the same.

For many of us there can be no 'grief timetable'. Some 'work through' sooner than others, but for those of us who are bereaved because it is our child who has died, grief is longer and more devastating than any other extreme trauma in our lives. However inevitable loss is to the human condition, the loss of a child is 'upside down'. Our instinct to be outlived by our daughters and sons has been violated.

We each operate on our own timetable; we cannot judge our progress or lack of it by anyone else, though the experience of others may well be useful to hear. And let's face it – grief is the most authentic expression of the child's importance when alive, and marks the vast emptiness of their no longer being in the world.

Pathological grieving

So is there such a thing as 'pathological grieving'? Quite possibly. There are people (am I one of them?) for whom the pain remains high and in whom there seems little transformation of the bond with the dead loved one. There are people for whom the past seems the only worthwhile time, a time when their child was alive. Some of us cling to our relationship with the dead person. We echo, probably unconsciously, the words of Jesus and become people 'of sorrow, and acquainted with grief'. In a sense, grief becomes our best friend. Trying to reconstruct the past is what I call the 'Gatsby syndrome'. In F. Scott Fitzgerald's *The Great Gatsby*, Jay Gatsby was convinced of one thing, the *only* thing of vital importance to him: that he could re-create a past time when the object of his obsession, Daisy, would be his perfect love once again. But what the reader discovers is that Daisy never was his perfect love in the first place.

It is not clear whether bereaved people becoming fixated to a time when the lost child was alive comes from the single event, or from a more complicated set of circumstances not directly associated with and possibly preceding the death.

One regular correspondent of TCF, a mother of several children who lost her teenage son more than a decade ago, has been unable to leave her house since his death. The letters and poems she sends in to the journal are always addressed to her son, telling him that she still cannot go out of the house but will keep trying for his sake to do so. One of the surviving children sends in regular messages to her brother and drawings of butterflies – the design, colours and messages are unvarying.

Suffice to say that there is no rush to construct new categories of the 'pathology' of grief. In the older model of grief, the stages/problems were not based on research or clinical experience, but on the cultural values from which that model sprang.

The heart of this book brings together the experiences of many different kinds of child bereavement and outlines a map of recovery. If, indeed, there is such a thing as a pathology of grief, it needs to be carefully studied and described, not used as a means of trying to prohibit or condemn people's individual 'grief journeys'.

Searching for answers

Some 'whys' may well have an answer, but here are some that don't:

- Why are there genetic defects?
- Why, when she was so healthy, was our baby stricken with an incurable disease?
- Why have I had a/another miscarriage?
- Why didn't I check her/him in the middle of the night?
- Why did she have to suffer so when we couldn't even explain things to her?
- Why did the car come round the corner just at that moment?
- Why didn't the medicine help?

- Why didn't doctors tell her the risks of her prescribed medication?
- Why did she/he take illegal drugs?
- Why was my son/daughter the one caught in the crossfire and killed?
- Why did the virus infect my baby?
- Why didn't my son/daughter feel safe to say the word 'queer'?
- Why are some people homosexual?
- Why did my child have to die?

Sometimes the answer is that there is no answer. If you are reading this book as a newly bereaved person, the following list of suggestions may seem daunting, especially when asking for anything at all can be an ordeal. But even if you feel you cannot ask for help, it may help you to read the list.

Ways of helping others to help you

Ask friends and relatives to:
- Phone you often. Explain that, especially after the early weeks and months, you'll need their calls.
- Fix a specific date with you – none of this 'we must get together for lunch sometime'. Remind them that you are going to have 'down' times, and that their patience would be appreciated.
- Feel free to talk about the loved one who has died – remind them that they don't need to avoid using the beloved's name.
- Understand that your appearance of 'doing well' may be deceptive because on the inside you hurt. Grief is painful beyond description; it is tricky, and it is exhausting.
- Care, but not to pity you . . . well, perhaps just a bit.
- Go walking with you. Walks promote conversation and help carry grief.

Let your friends and relatives know that:
- You are still in command and can think for yourself.
- It is appropriate to cry and show that they care. Crying together is better than avoiding the subject.
- It is all right to be silent. A squeeze or a hug is often more important than words.
- You are open to social invitations, but not to be upset if you decline.

(Revised and reproduced with thanks to the Southwestern Manitoba chapter of TCF. Original version by Ruth Jean Loewinsohn, TCF, Mount Vernon, Ohio, USA, February 1997.)

More helpful suggestions

The following ideas will be helpful to grieving families, as well as those trying to care for bereaved people:

- Natural support systems for families and communities. People need concrete assistance, support over a period of time – especially *after* the first raw weeks and months – and we need people who will listen and believe in the need for ongoing care and concern. We need people who can share the bond with the dead loved one, and make that bond part of our ongoing relationship with the surviving loved one. No individual or family should have to deal with a death and the subsequent grief alone. People in thriving church and social communities have an advantage in this respect.

- Mutual and self-help organizations – such as TCF, CRUSE, and similar organizations for solo parents, adopted children, stepchildren – have pioneered the way. As we saw earlier, TCF was first formed because an imaginative hospital chaplain saw that two sets of parents would be able to legitimate one another's experience in a form not available any other way. These organizations are based on peer support and the uncommonly common sense of simply 'being there' for one another.

  Survivors can express themselves, begin to see a future, and to find role models in people who have lived through their grief and made something new from the ruins. We may then move from being a recipient of help to being a helper.

- Adopted children need to know that it is acceptable to search for birth parents and to learn the practical details involved in conducting the search.

- Holidays, once cherished as special family times, can literally loom like a dark cloud after losing a child. Parents may find that including memories of the dead child helps.

- Helping others is one of the ways of finding a new meaning for the pain we have suffered. In my personal experience, it has been the best way.

- Help your body. Look after it so that it doesn't come back to bite you.
- Lobby for justice if the circumstances of a loved one's death requires it – for example, families of children killed by drunken/ careless drivers. In the case of medication and drug-related deaths, draw attention to the dangers of drugs. Campaign for the pharmaceutical companies to warn doctors and patients of the dangers of particular drugs.

Being creative with grief

It's sometimes difficult to identify exactly what gives us strength – perhaps even admitting to a strength feels like an injustice to our dead child, or that we are being rushed through our grief. Suggestions that do in fact help us when some time has elapsed may be taken as an outrage in the numbing early times following the death of our child. Here are some ideas that may help when you feel ready:

Needlework

When her son died of cancer, a friend's grandmother remembered that he kept every handkerchief, tie and cravat he'd ever owned. She then decided to make quilted cushions for each of the grandchildren from the material.

Grief writing

I remain in awe of the poets and essayists whose response to the death of their child brought forth writing of passion, beauty and encouragement, speaking not only for themselves but to others. It is difficult to overestimate the value of this process, and I view the greatest honour of editing *Compassion* for TCF as the receiving of these writings, corresponding with the authors and publishing their work. The joy of being able to put their words into print for other bereaved parents is very special. Thank you, fellow bereaved parents, for writing from your heart and to the hearts of so many others.

Private journal

This is in essence what Una, my spiritual director, suggested I keep after Caitlin's death. However, I found I couldn't do this, although I did try, and managed occasional random chicken scratches of despair in the back of my filofax, and in my journal, which became an erratic but important measuring stick for later on. I recall dear Amy Eldon's cry from the heart (see Chapter 4) that she felt afraid because she was beginning to forget things about her brother. Her mother Kathy's suggested solution was a journal of detail, recalling Dan's death, the funeral, but also humour, memories, photos, letters, favourite sayings. These documents can become lovely mementos for sharing with surviving family and friends (Eldon and Eldon, 1998).

Writing a letter to our dead child can be helpful. We can tell them what we wish we had or hadn't done or said before they died. We can let them know that we love them always and, if appropriate, try to say 'Goodbye'. Here are some further ideas:

- Writing poetry or articles.
- Music.
- Media work.
- Planting a garden of remembrance.
- Visual things: compiling memory boxes (especially for babies); making collages.
- Paintings.
- Art: cards, jewellery, bookmarks, candles.
- Quilts, wall hangings, using fabrics from child's belongings.
- Cooking and baking bread.
- Interior decorating. Redecorate a sibling's room to reassure them of their continued importance in the family – maybe decorate other rooms too.
- Befriending. Try to invest in relationships, with friends of the dead child. Painful but often helpful.
- Fundraising for causes related to our child's death.
- Joining/organizing a charity to reach out to others.
- If relevant, begin a self-help group.
- Write a book. If you can't find a publisher (notoriously difficult), you might try self-publishing. But don't print too many copies! And remember, a book is not a child. Expect to hear from friends that this will be a huge catharsis for you. Smile mysteriously.

'Witness' and 'advocate'

In putting this book together I have struggled with many 'official' bereavement words and phrases that I find objectionable. The obvious ones – closure, completion, recovery, letting go, 'getting over it' – have been discussed already. But I have also struggled on a more subtle level with the word 'victim' when applied to grieving parents and siblings, and I have tussled too with the word 'survivor'. Although I can see the legal value of describing as 'victims' bereaved parents whose child died in dubious/violent/mysterious circumstances, the use of the word does not work for me, because the real victim is the person who died; we who are left behind to live on have suffered and continue to suffer, but are we the appropriate objects of victimhood in these cases? Am I being too harsh? I recall Margaret Atwood's words in her novel *Surfacing*: 'This above all. To refuse to be a victim.'

My hesitation about being a 'survivor' is more pernickety. Certainly I have survived the death of my child. But so what? Is that the point? To go around saying 'I'm still here, I'm still here'? This is missing the point. The difficult part is the very fact that I am 'surviving' (outliving) my child – which of course goes against all our normal expectations as parents. It is the wrong way round.

I prefer the words 'witness' and 'advocate'. It is as someone who has 'seen or known, who has explored new terrain, and is therefore competent to give evidence concerning it' that I get up every morning and face each new day. It is as an advocate and explorer, 'one who defends, describes or supports someone or something'. The 'someone', being you, the reader, the 'something' being the importance of discovering ways to honour our dead children in the lives we live. We witnesses come armed variously; we must record every leaf, path, tree. We continue to build bridges of love.

Helpful Contacts

Al-Anon Family Groups UK (incorporating Alateen for young people)
General Service Office, 61 Great Dover Street, London SE1 4YF. Tel. 020 7403 0888.
E-mail: alanonuk@aol.com
Websites: www.hexnet.co.uk/alanon
www.al-anon.alateen.org
Scotland: Al-Anon Information Centre, Mansfield Park Unit 6, 22 Mansfield Street, Partick, Glasgow G11 5QP. Tel. 0141 339 8884.
Northern Ireland: Al-Anon Info Centre, Peace House, 224 Lisburn Road, Belfast BT9 6GE. Tel. 028 9068 2368
Eire: Al-Anon Info Centre, Room 5, Capel Street, Dublin 1. Tel. 00 353 1873 2699.

APRIL (Adverse Psychiatric Reactions Information Link)
PO Box 2082, Woodford Green, Essex IG8 0GS. Tel. 01992 813111.
E-mail: info@april.co.uk
Website: www.april.org.uk

Ashley Jolly Sudden Adult Death Trust
Anne Jolly, SADS UK, 22 Rowhedge, Brentwood, Essex CM13 2TS. Tel. 01277 230642.
E-mail: info@sadsuk.org
Website: www.sadsuk.org
Support for relatives of those who have died from cardiac failure.

AVMA (Action for Victims of Medical Accidents)
44 High Street, Croydon, Surrey CR0 1YB. Tel. 020 8685 8333.
E-mail: admin@avma.org.uk

Bereavement Counselling Service
Dublin Street, Baldoyle, Dublin 13, Ireland. Tel. 00 353 1839 1766 (Monday to Friday, 9.15 a.m. to 1 p.m.).
E-mail: bereavement@eircom.net

BODY (British Organ Donor Society)

1 The Rookery, Balsham, Cambridge CB1 6DL. Tel. 01223 893636.
E-mail: body@argonet.co.uk
Website: www.users.argonet.co.uk/body

Bristol and District Tranquilliser Project

88 Henleaze Road, Henleaze, Bristol BS9 4JY. Tel./fax: 0117 962 2509 (office); 0117 934 9950 (helpline).
Provides information and advice for those who feel they have been on medication for too long.

British Association for Counselling and Psychotherapy

BACP House, 35–37 Albert Street, Rugby CV21 2SG. Tel. 0870 443 5252.
E-mail: bacp@bacp.co.uk
Website: www.bacp.co.uk

Child Bereavement Trust

Aston House, West Wycombe, Bucks HP14 3AG. Tel. 0845 357 1000.
E-mail: enquiries@childbereavement.org.uk
Website: www.childbereavement.org.uk
A national UK charity founded to improve the support offered by professionals to grieving families.

Child Death Helpline

Tel. 0800 282986.
E-mail: contact@childdeathhelpline.org
Website: www.childdeathhelpline.org.uk
Based at Alder Hey Children's Hospital in Liverpool and Great Ormond Street Children's Hospital in London.

ChildLine

45 Folgate Street, London E1 6GL. Tel. 0800 1111 (helpline).
Website: www.childline.org.uk
Provides bereavement support and other help for children.

CRUSE Bereavement Care

126 Sheen Road, Richmond, Surrey TW9 1UR. Tel. 020 8939 9530 (office); 0870 167 1677 (helpline).
Email: helpline@crusebereavementcare.org.uk
Website: www.crusebereavementcare.org.uk
Provides free information and advice to anyone affected by a death.

Down's Heart Bereavement Group
17 Cantilupe Close, Eaton Bray, Dunstable, Beds LU6 2EA. Tel. 01525 220379.
E-mail: downs_heart_group@msn.com
Website: www.downs-heart.downsnet.org
Supports families of Down's syndrome children, especially those with heart defects.

Foundation for Black Bereaved Families
11 Kingston Square, Salters Hill, London SE19 1JE. Tel. 020 8661 7228.

Foundation for the Study of Infant Deaths (FSID)
Artillery House, 11–19 Artillery Row, London SW1P 1RT. Tel. 020 7222 8001.
Email: fsid@sids.org.uk
Website: www.sids.org.uk/fsid

Gingerbread
7 Sovereign Close, Sovereign Court, London E1W 3HW. Tel. 020 7488 9300 (office); 0800 018 4318 (Freephone advice line, Mondays to Fridays, 9 a.m.–5 p.m.)
E-mail: office@gingerbread.org.uk
Website: www.gingerbread.org.uk
Provides help for lone-parent families.

Graeme Peart
Saxlingham Place, Holt, Norfolk NR25 7JZ. Tel. 01328 830135
E-mail: jgpeart@aol.com
A bereaved father and an experienced independent litigation solicitor specializing in fatal litigation cases, Graeme is author of *Death of a Child and the Legal System* (details available via www.tcf.org.uk/leaflets). His phone number is a nationwide legal helpline, open at all times for bereaved parents, families and friends.

Grandparents Association
Moot House, The Stow, Harlow, Essex CM20 3AG. Tel. 01279 428040 (office); 01279 444964 (helpline).
E-mail: info@grandparents-association.org.uk
Website: www.grandparents-federation.org.uk

Hearing Voices Network
91 Oldham Street, Manchester M4 1LW.

Founded by Rufus May, this network provides support for people seeking to find ways of coping with hearing voices.

Jessie's Fund
Lesley Schatzberger, Jessie's Fund, 10 Bootham Terrace, York YO30 7DH. Tel./fax 01904 658189.
E-mail: info@jessiesfund.org.uk
E-mail outside the UK: jessiesfund@aol.com
Website: www.jessiesfund.org.uk
Helps life-limited children all over the United Kingdom through music therapy: the majority cannot speak, and music provides a vital means of communication and expression for them.

Jewish Bereavement Counselling Service
8/10 Forty Avenue, Wembley, Middlesex HA9 8JW. Tel. 020 8385 1874.
E-mail: jbcs@jvisit.org.uk
Website: www.jvisit.org.uk/jbcs

Kidscape, 2 Grosvenor Gardens, London SW1W 0DH. Tel. 020 7730 3300 (office); 08451 205 204 (helpline: Monday to Friday, 10 a.m.–4 p.m.).
Website: www.kidscape.org.uk

Lauren's Link
Annette Rodgers, Dovedale House, 73 Wilson Street, Suites 5, 6 and 7, Derby DE1 1PL. Tel. 01332 362744.
E-mail: info@laurenslink.org.uk
Website: www.laurenslink.org.uk
For families with children troubled by drug addiction.

Lesbian and Gay Bereavement Project
C/o Terrence Higgins Trust Counselling Services, c/o London Lighthouse, 111–117 Lancaster Road, London W11 1QT. Tel. 020 7816 0330 (switchboard); 020 7403 5969 (helpline, Tuesdays to Thursdays only, 7.30 p.m.–10.30 p.m.).

Macmillan CancerLine, Macmillan Cancer Relief
89 Albert Embankment, London SE1 7UQ. Tel. 020 7840 7840 (office); 0808 808 2020 (helpline Monday to Friday, 9 a.m.–6 p.m).
E-mail: cancerline@macmillan.co.uk
Website: www.cancerlink.org

MIND (National Association for Mental Health)

Granta House, 15–19 Broadway, Stratford, London E15 4BQ. Tel. 020 8519 2122 (office); 0845 766 0163 (helpline; Mindinfoline).
E-mail: contact@mind.org.uk
Website: www.mind.org.uk
Includes information and advice service.

Muscular Dystrophy Group

77–11 Prescott Place, London SW4 6BS. Tel. 020 7720 8055.
E-mail: info@muscular-dystrophy.org
Website: www.muscular-dystrophy.org

Narcotics Anonymous

UK Service Office, 202 City Road, London EC1V 2PH. Tel. 020 7251 4007 (office); 020 7736 0009 (helpline).
E-mail: ukso@ukna.org (for general information)
E-mail helpline: helpline@ukna.org

National Association of Bereavement Services

2nd Floor, 4 Pinchin Street London E1 1SA. Tel. 020 7709 9090 (helpline).

Natural Death Centre

6 Blackstock Mews, Blackstock Road, London N4 2BT. Tel. 020 7359 8391.
E-mail: ndc@alberyfoundation.org
Website: www.naturaldeath.org
Alternative website: www.worldtrans.org/naturaldeath.html
Supports those dying at home and their carers, and gives very good information on resources for alternative funerals.

National Stepfamily Association

Chapel House, 18 Hatton Place, London EC1N 8RU. Tel. 020 7209 2460.
E-mail: tnsa@aukonline.co.uk

PAPYRUS

Rossendale GH, Union Road, Rawstenstall, Lancs BB4 6NE. Tel. 01706 214449.
E-mail: admin@papyrus-uk.org
Website: www.papyrus-uk.org
Helps those seeking to prevent suicides.

Prozac and Antidepressants Alert Networks (PANTS UK)
E-mail: pants.uk@virgin.net
Includes information and advice service.

Retained Organs Commission
Tel. 0800 838 909 (helpline).

Rethink
30 Tabernacle Street, London EC2A 4DD. Tel. 020 7330 9100/01
(office); 020 8974 6814 (helpline, Monday to Friday,10 a.m.–
3 p.m.).
E-mail: info@rethink.org.uk
Website: www.rethink.org
Encourages working together to help those affected by severe mental
illness, including schizophrenia, to recover a better quality of life.

Road Peace
PO Box 2579, London NW10 3PW. Tel. 020 8838 5102 (Kim
Worts).
E-mail: info@roadpeace.co.uk
Website: www.roadpeace.org
Supports road-crash victims and campaigns to reduce danger to all
road users.

SADS UK *See* Ashley Jolly Sudden Adult Death Trust.

Samaritans
The Upper Mill, Kingston Road, Ewell, Surrey KT17 2AF. Tel. 020
8394 8300 (office); 08457 90 90 90 (national UK helpline); 00 353
1850 60 90 90 (national Eire helpline).
E-mail: admin@samaritans.org
Website: www.samaritans.org.uk
Samaritans offer a trained person to talk to who will give support.
There are over 180 branches in the United Kingdom which are open
24 hours a day.

SAMM (Support After Murder and Manslaughter)
Cranmer House, 39 Brixton Road, London SW9 6DZ. Tel. 020 7735
3838.
E-mail: enquiries@samm.org.uk
Website: www.samm.org.uk
National organization for families bereaved through murder and
manslaughter.

SANDS (Stillbirth and Neonatal Deaths Society)
28 Portland Place, London W1B 1LY. Tel. 020 7436 7940 (office:
10 a.m.–5 p.m., Mondays to Fridays); 020 7436 5881 (helpline:
10 a.m.–3 p.m., Mondays to Fridays).
E-mail: support@uk-sands.org
Website: www.uk-sands.org

SIBBS (Support in Bereavement for Brothers and Sisters)
See The Compassionate Friends.

SOBS (Survivors of Bereavement by Suicide)
National Office, Centre 88, Saner Street, Hull HU3 2TR. Tel. 01482
610728 (office); 0870 241 3337 (helpline).
E-mail(administrative): sobs.admin@care4free.net (support)
sobs.support@care4free.net
Website: www.uk-sobs.org.uk
For anyone bereaved by a suicide.

SOS (Shadow of Suicide)
See The Compassionate Friends.

SSAFA Forces Help
19 Queen Elizabeth Street, London SE1 2LP. Tel. 020 7403 8783.
E-mail: info@ssafa.org.uk
Website: www.ssafa.org.uk
National charity helping both serving and ex-service men, women
and their families in need.

Terrence Higgins Trust
52–54 Gray's Inn Road, London WC1X 8JU. Tel. 020 7831 0330
(office); 0845 1221 200 (national helpline).
E-mail: info@tht.org.uk
Website: www.tht.org.uk
For sufferers from HIV/AIDS and those who care for them.

The Compassionate Friends UK (TCF)
53 North Street, Bristol BS3 1EN. Tel. 0845 1203 785 (office); 0845
1232 304 (helpline).
E-mail: info@tcf.org.uk
Website: www.tcf.org.uk
The original and internationally affiliated charity of bereaved parents
and families offering understanding, support and encouragement to

others after the death of a child or children. The Shadow of Suicide group (SOS) brings together parents who are similarly bereaved. Support in Bereavement for Brothers and Sisters (SIBBS) is also a part of TCF, as is Families Bereaved by Homicide (FBbH).

Victim Support
Cranmer House, 39 Brixton Road, London SW9 6DZ. Tel. 020 7735 9166.
E-mail: contact@victimsupport.org.uk
Website: www.victimsupport.org

Useful websites

AARP (formerly American Association of Retired Persons) is for the over-50s. Helpful contacts and information on bereavement: www.aarp.org/griefandloss/about.html

www.bereavement.org is an 'e-book' resource for those who grieve and those who provide support for the bereaved.

The organization Genelex (www.genelux.com) works in the field of DNA testing and its link website (www.healthanddna.com) provides valuable information on the most up-to-date information about averting adverse drug reactions.

GriefNet.org is an internet community of persons dealing with grief, death, and major loss. There are 47 e-mail support groups and two websites: the other website, KIDSAID (kidsaid.com), provides a safe environment for children and their parents and carers to find information and ask questions.

If I Should Die is a website dedicated to providing as much practical information and support as possible in one easy place: www.ifishoulddie.co.uk

Centering Corporation, TCF USA's recommended supplier for grief resources. Publishes available resources covering such areas as: children and grief; adults and grief; infant loss; plus general information.
www.centering.org/mission.html

Hospices in the United Kingdom and Ireland: an up-to-date list of

hospice information pages can be reached at:
www.hauraki.co.uk/hospice_uk

Legal matters can be found at:
http://www.desktoplawyer.freeserve.net/law/

SIDS (Sudden Infant Death Syndrome)
Network http://sids-network.org/
A site that deals not only with stillbirth and neonatal deaths, but also discusses issues such as sibling grief.

Memorials

Memorials by Artists
C/o Harriet Frazer MBE, Snape Priory, Snape, Saxmundham, Suffolk IP17 1SA. Tel. 01728 688934.
E-mail: enquiries@memorialsbyartists.co.uk
Website: www.memorialsbyartists.co.uk
A registered charity owned by the Memorial Arts Charity.

Will and Lottie O'Leary, Memorial Masons and Carvers
Upper House, Knucklas, Knighton, Powys SD7 1PN. Tel./fax 01547 528792.
Website: www.stonecarving.co.uk
Highly recommended artists who assisted me with the choice and decoration of Caitlin's headstone. Beautiful stones, designed and worked by hand.

References and Further Reading

Ainsworth-Smith, I. (2002), 'Grief', *The New Dictionary of Pastoral Studies*, SPCK.

Albery, N., Elliott, G., and Elliott, J. (eds) (1997), *The New Natural Death Handbook*, Ebury.

Alvarez, A. (1971), *The Savage God: A Study of Suicide*, Weidenfeld & Nicolson.

Baugher, Bob (1998), in *We Need Not Walk Alone*, TCF USA.

Baxter, L. (2002), 'For our spiritual Warrior', *TCF Newsletter*, issue no. 134. Linda's poem is from her book, *Losing Timo*, to be published by Hanno Welsh Women's Press in 2005.

Bell, Margaret (2001), 'A Postmortem and Some Foxgloves', *TCF Newsletter*, issue no. 127.

Brown, M., and Ferguson-Brown, H. (2001) (video series), *The Suicide of Young People and its impact on the Family*, University of Lincoln, 2001.

Clarke, P. (1999), *The Story of The Compassionate Friends*, TCF.

Dominica, F. (1997), *Just My Reflection: Helping parents to do things their way when their child dies*. Darton, Longman & Todd.

Dunn, M. (2000), *The Good Death Guide: Everything you wanted to know but were afraid to ask*, How To Books.

Eldon, K. (1997), *The Journey is the Destination: The Journals of Dan Eldon*, Booth-Clibborn Editions.

Eldon, K., and Eldon, A. (1999), *Angel Catcher: A Grieving Journal*, Chronicle Books.

Farrant, A. (1998), *Sibling Bereavement: Helping Children Cope with Loss*, Continuum.

Grollman, E. A. (1988), *Suicide: Prevention, Intervention, Postvention* (2nd edn), Beacon Press.

Harvey, M. (2001), 'Talking About Suicide with Young Children', *TCF Newsletter*, issue no. 127.

Hayworth, M. (1989), 'Thoughts on Befriending', *TCF Newsletter*.

Healy, D. (2002), 'Depression', *The New Dictionary of Pastoral Studies*, SPCK.

Healy, D. (2003), *Let Them Eat Prozac*, James Lorimer & Company Ltd.

Helen, M. (2002), *Coping with Suicide*, Sheldon Press.

Hickman, M. W. (1999), *Healing after Loss: Daily Meditations for Working Through Grief*, Avon Books.

Hill, K. (1995), *The Long Sleep: Young People and Suicide*, Virago Press.

James, J. W., and Friedman, R. (1998), *The Grief Recovery Handbook: The Action Program for Moving Beyond Death, Divorce, and Other Losses*, HarperCollins.

Jamison, K. R. (1999), *Night Falls Fast: Understanding Suicide*, Macmillan.

Jones, E. (2001), *Bibliotherapy for Bereaved Children*, Jessica Kingsley.

Klass, D., Silverman, P. R., and Nickman, S. L. (eds) (1996), *Continuing Bonds: New Understandings of Grief*, Taylor & Francis.

Kübler-Ross, E., *Death is of Vital Importance: on Life, Death and Life After*. Station Hill Press, Barrytown, 1994.

Kushner, H. S. (1989), *Self-Destruction in the Promised Land: A Psychocultural Biology of American Suicide*, Rutgers University Press.

Kushner, H. S. (1992), *When Bad Things Happen to Good People*, Pan.

Lager, E., with Wagner, S. (1997), *Knowing Why Changes Nothing*, Options.

Lewis, C. S. (1961), *A Grief Observed*, Faber and Faber.

Lukas, C., and Seiden, H. (1997), Silent Grief: *Living in the Wake of Suicide*, 2nd edn, Jason Aronson Inc.

MacLeish, A. (1958), *J.B.: A Play in Verse*, Houghton Mifflin.

McGough, R. (2002), 'Sad Music', in *Everyday Eclipses*, Viking.

Marsden, J. (1999), *A Message for the 21st Century*, Ticktock Publishing.

Miller, J. (ed.) (1992), *On Suicide: Great Writers on the Ultimate Question*, Chronicle Books.

Mirren, E. (ed.) (1995), *Our Children: Coming to Terms with the Loss of a Child: Parents' Own Stories*, Hodder & Stoughton.

Neil, L. (1999), 'Grieving and Driving', in *The Landscape of Grief*, ed. Pat Neil, The Compassionate Friends.

Nuland, S. (1997), *How We Die*, Vintage.

Picardie, J. (2002), *If the Spirit Moves You: Love and Life After Death*, Picador.

Rando, T. (1991), *How to Go On Living When Someone You Love Dies*, Bantam.

Ratna, L. (2002), 'Behaviour Therapy', *The New Dictionary of Pastoral Studies*, SPCK.

Riches, G., and Dawson, P. (2000), *An Intimate Loneliness: Supporting Bereaved Parents and Siblings*, Open University Press.

Rowe, D. (2001), *Depression: The Way Out of Your Prison*, 2nd edn, Brunner-Routledge.

Schiff, H. S. (1999), *The Bereaved Parent*, Souvenir Press.

Schneidman, E. S. (ed.) (1984), *Death: Current Perspectives*. William C. Brown.

Sieff, B. (2003), in *We Need Not Walk Alone*, TCF USA, Spring.

Stevenson, N. C., and Straffon, C. H. (1981), *When Your Child Dies: Finding the Meaning in Mourning*, Philomel Press, Theo Publishing Co.

Storkey, E. (1999), *Losing a Child: Finding a Path through the Pain*. Lion Publishing.

TCF (1997), *On Inquests* (England and Wales) (leaflet).

TCF (1998), *Our Surviving Children* (leaflet).

Tonkin, L. (1997), *Bereavement Care*, a CRUSE publication.

Tyson, J. N. (1998), *Common Threads of Teenage Grief: A Handbook for Healing*, Helm Publishing.

Walton, C. (1996), *When There Are No Words: Finding your way to cope with loss and grief*, Pathfinder Publishing.

Walton, C. (2003), Keynote Speech to TCF (USA) National Conference, Atlanta, Georgia, 6 July 2003. Published in *Compassion*, issue no. 137.

Wells, R. (1988), *Helping Children Cope with Grief: Facing a death in the family*, Sheldon Press.

Wertheimer, A. (2001), *A Special Scar: The Experiences of People Bereaved by Suicide*, 2nd edn, Routledge.

White-Bowden, S. (1985), *Everything to Live For*, Pocket Books.

Williams, J. G. (1965), *On the Death of a Child* (booklet), SPCK.

Wilson, G., with McCreary, A. 1990), *Marie: A Story from Enniskillen*, Marshall Pickering.

Index